~ *All Time* ~

FAMILY FAVORITES™

CHICKEN & TURKEY

PUBLICATIONS INTERNATIONAL, LTD.

Microwave Cooking: Microwave ovens may vary in wattage. The microwave cooking times given in this publication are approximate. Use the cooking times as guidelines and check for doneness before adding more time. Consult manufacturer's instructions for suitable microwave-safe dishes.

— Contents —

— Chicken & Turkey Basics —

Few foods offer a better selection for everyday cooking than chicken and turkey. Economical, versatile and readily available, their universal appeal makes them a winning choice for almost any occasion—from a casual picnic in the park to a romantic candlelight dinner for two. Here are some helpful tips for selecting and preparing chicken and turkey.

WHAT'S AVAILABLE

Whole chickens and turkeys are readily available and usually have the neck and giblets wrapped separately and placed inside the cavity. The most common type of whole chicken is a broiler-fryer, weighing from 1½ to 3½ pounds. The meat is tender, mildly flavored and best when broiled, fried, roasted or sautéed. Whole, young turkeys commonly range in weight from 10 to 20 pounds. Turkeys up to 25 pounds are best when roasted; larger, older turkeys need to be stewed in order to become tender. No longer served just at Thanksgiving, this bird has mild flavor that makes it an appealing choice throughout the year.

Chicken and turkey pieces are available to suit a variety of taste preferences, budgets, cooking styles and cuisines. Packaged legs have the thighs and drumsticks attached. Thighs and drumsticks are sometimes cut apart and packaged separately. Chicken and turkey breasts are available whole or split into halves, with or without the bone. Wings can also be purchased separately. Chicken drumettes, which are disjointed wing sections, are a popular choice for many appetizers, and boneless chicken tenders provide a quick start for

many recipes. Boneless turkey roasts and turkey tenderloins are perfect for when a whole turkey is too much.

Ground chicken and turkey, now commonly found in the poultry case, are popular as low-fat replacements for ground beef or pork. Be sure to check the label before purchasing. Some brands add dark meat and skin, which increase the fat and cholesterol content. Turkey breakfast links and Italian sausages, both mild and hot, are other lower-fat products you may wish to try.

STORING CHICKEN AND TURKEY

Store fresh, raw chicken and turkey pieces in their original wrap for up to two days in the coldest part of the refrigerator. Leftover cooked poultry keeps three to four days when tightly wrapped and refrigerated. Most poultry can be frozen in its original packaging safely for up to two months. For longer freezing, double-wrap or rewrap with freezer paper, foil or plastic wrap for an airtight package, then label, date and freeze.

Before repackaging and freezing a whole chicken or turkey for longer storage, remove the giblets from the cavity of the bird. Rinse the giblets under running water and pat dry with paper towels. Trim any excess fat from the bird. Tightly wrap the bird and giblets in separate packages using freezer-strength plastic, paper or foil. Label and date each package, then freeze. A whole chicken or turkey can be frozen for up to one year; smaller pieces, such as breasts and tenderloins, can be frozen for up to three months. Larger cuts and skin-on parts can be frozen for six months.

Thaw frozen chicken and turkey pieces in their original or freezer wrap in the refrigerator. Thawing times vary depending on the size of the poultry pieces and the package. A general guideline is to allow 24 hours of thawing time for a 5-pound whole chicken; allow about five hours per pound for thawing chicken and turkey pieces. To reduce thawing time, freeze poultry in smaller, meal-size portions. To thaw a whole turkey, place the wrapped turkey on a tray in the refrigerator. Allow five hours per pound to thaw completely. If time is short, place the wrapped turkey in the sink and cover with cold water. Allow one half hour per pound for the turkey to thaw completely. Change the water every 30 minutes. Never thaw chicken or turkey at room temperature, because this promotes bacterial growth.

CHICKEN AND TURKEY PREPARATION TIPS

- Before handling raw poultry, make sure the cutting board, utensils and your hands are clean. Afterward, wash the cutting board, knife and your hands in hot, sudsy water. This eliminates the risk of contaminating other foods with harmful salmonella bacteria that is often present in raw poultry.

- Poultry should always be cooked completely before eating. You should never cook poultry partially and then store it to be finished later, because this promotes bacterial growth.

- Never let cooked poultry stand at room temperature for more than two hours. In hot weather, reduce the time to one hour.

- Spoon stuffing loosely into the body and neck cavities of a whole chicken or turkey just prior to roasting. Never stuff the bird ahead of time. Remove the stuffing from the bird immediately after roasting.

CUTTING A WHOLE CHICKEN INTO HALVES AND QUARTERS

1. Place chicken breast side down on cutting board with neck end away from you. Working from neck to tail, cut along one side of backbone, cutting as close to bone as possible. Cut down other side of backbone; remove backbone.

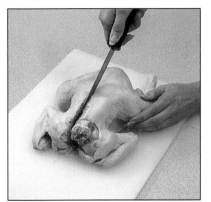

2. Remove breastbone (see "Skinning and Deboning a Whole Chicken Breast," steps 1–7).

3. Turn chicken skin side up. Cut lengthwise down center of chicken to split into halves.

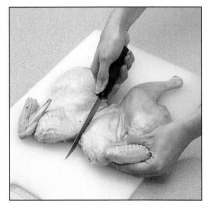

4. To cut into quarters, cut through skin separating thighs from breast.

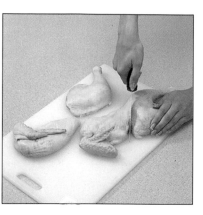

3. Grasp breast with both hands and gently bend both sides backward to snap breastbone.

SKINNING AND DEBONING A WHOLE CHICKEN BREAST

1. Freeze chicken breast until firm but not hard. (However, do not refreeze thawed chicken.) Grasp skin with clean cotton kitchen towel and pull away from meat; discard skin. When finished skinning chicken breast, launder towel before using again.

4. With fingers, work along both sides of breastbone to loosen triangular keel bone; pull out bone.

2. Place breast meaty side down on cutting board. Cut small slit through membrane and cartilage at the V of the neck end.

5. With tip of sharp knife, cut along both sides of cartilage at end of breastbone. Remove cartilage.

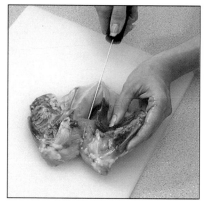

6. Slip point of knife under long rib bone on one side of breast. Cut and scrape meat from rib bone, pulling bones away from meat.

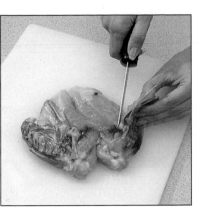

9. To remove white tendon from each side of breast, cut enough meat away from each tendon so you can grasp it (use paper towel for firmer grasp). Remove tendon.

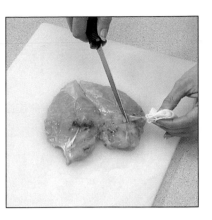

7. Cut meat away from collarbone. Remove bones. Repeat procedure to debone other side of breast.

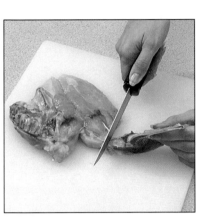

10. Turn breast meaty side up. If desired, remove chicken tenders from thickest edge of each breast half and reserve for another use. Trim any loosened remaining connective tissue, if needed. Cut whole chicken breast lengthwise into halves, if desired.

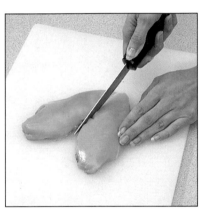

8. Remove wishbones of chicken breasts that have been cut from whole chickens in your home kitchen. Cut meat away from wishbone at neck end of breast. Grasp wishbone and pull it out of breast.

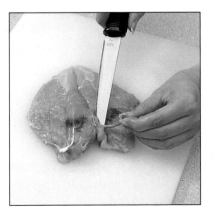

DONENESS TESTS

- For whole chickens and turkeys, a meat thermometer inserted into the thickest part of the thigh, but not near the bone or fat, should register 180°F to 185°F. If the bird is stuffed, insert the thermometer into the center of the body cavity; when the stuffing registers 165°F, the chicken or turkey should be done.

- A fork inserted into a chicken or turkey piece should go in with ease and the juices should run clear. The meat and juices nearest the bone may still be a little pink; however, the meat should no longer be pink in the center. Boneless pieces are done when the centers are no longer pink; test this by cutting into the piece with a knife.

APPETIZERS & SALADS

TURKEY AVOCADO BOATS

3 large ripe avocados, halved and pitted
6 tablespoons lemon juice
¾ cup mayonnaise
1½ tablespoons grated onion
¼ teaspoon celery salt
¼ teaspoon garlic powder
Salt and pepper to taste
2 cups diced cooked turkey or chicken
½ cup (2 ounces) shredded sharp Cheddar
  cheese
Snipped chives (optional)

Preheat oven to 350°F. Sprinkle each avocado half with 1 tablespoon lemon juice. Combine mayonnaise, onion, celery salt, garlic powder, salt and pepper in medium bowl. Stir in turkey; mix well. Drain any excess lemon juice from avocado halves. Fill avocado halves with turkey mixture; sprinkle with cheese. Arrange filled avocado halves in single layer in baking dish. Pour water into same dish to depth of ½ inch. Bake filled avocado halves 15 minutes or until cheese melts. Garnish with chives, if desired.

Makes 6 servings

CHICKEN PIZZA

> 1 package (8 ounces) refrigerated crescent rolls
> ¼ cup vegetable oil
> 4 boneless skinless chicken breasts, coarsely chopped
> 1 large green bell pepper, sliced into thin rings
> 1 large onion, sliced into thin rings
> ½ pound sliced mushrooms
> ½ cup sliced pitted ripe olives
> 1 can (10½ ounces) pizza sauce with cheese
> ¼ cup grated Parmesan cheese
> 1 teaspoon garlic salt
> 1 teaspoon dried oregano leaves
> 2 cups (8 ounces) shredded mozzarella cheese

Preheat oven to 425°F. Separate dough into 8 triangles. Press triangles into greased 12-inch pizza pan, covering bottom of pan completely. Seal seams. Heat oil in large skillet over medium-high heat. Add chicken, bell pepper, onion, mushrooms and olives. Cook and stir 5 minutes or until chicken is no longer pink in center.

Spread pizza sauce over dough. Spoon chicken mixture over top. Sprinkle with Parmesan cheese, garlic salt and oregano. Top with mozzarella cheese. Bake 20 minutes or until crust is golden brown. Cut into wedges to serve.

Makes 8 to 10 servings

Favorite recipe from **National Broiler Council**

DIJON ASPARAGUS CHICKEN SALAD

> 1 cup HELLMANN'S® or BEST FOODS® Real Mayonnaise or Light Reduced Calorie Mayonnaise Dressing
> 2 tablespoons Dijon-style mustard
> 2 tablespoons lemon juice
> 1 teaspoon salt
> ½ teaspoon black pepper
> 6 ounces tricolor twist or spiral pasta, cooked, rinsed with cold water and drained
> 1 pound boneless skinless chicken breasts, cooked and cubed
> 1 package (10 ounces) frozen asparagus spears, thawed and cut into 2-inch pieces
> 1 red bell pepper, cut into 1-inch squares

In large bowl, combine mayonnaise, mustard, lemon juice, salt and black pepper. Stir in pasta, chicken, asparagus and bell pepper. Cover; refrigerate at least 1 hour before serving.

Makes 6 servings

Chicken Pizza

MONTMORENCY CHERRY CHICKEN SALAD

  3 nectarines or peaches, divided
  3 cups cubed cooked chicken
  2 cups tart red Montmorency cherries,*
    pitted
 1½ cups sliced celery
  2 tablespoons sliced green onion
  1 cup mayonnaise
  ¼ cup sour cream
  2 tablespoons honey
  1 teaspoon lemon juice
  ¼ to ½ teaspoon curry powder
  ⅛ teaspoon ground ginger
    Salt to taste
  ½ cup slivered almonds, toasted, divided
    Boston or Bibb lettuce leaves

*If fresh Montmorency cherries are unavailable, substitute any fresh sour cherries. If fresh cherries are unavailable, substitute an equal amount of frozen pitted cherries. Thaw and drain cherries well.

Slice 1 nectarine; combine with chicken, cherries, celery and green onion in large bowl. Combine mayonnaise, sour cream, honey, lemon juice, curry powder, ginger and salt in small bowl; mix well. Pour mayonnaise mixture over chicken mixture; toss to coat. Cover; refrigerate at least 1 hour before serving.

Stir all but 1 tablespoon almonds into salad just before serving; arrange salad on lettuce-lined plates. Slice remaining 2 nectarines; arrange around salad. Sprinkle salad with remaining 1 tablespoon almonds.   *Makes 6 servings*

Favorite recipe from **New York Cherry Growers Association, Inc.**

CAJUN–STYLE CHICKEN NUGGETS

  1 envelope LIPTON® Recipe Secrets® Onion
    or Onion-Mushroom Soup Mix
  ½ cup dry bread crumbs
 1½ teaspoons chili powder
  1 teaspoon ground cumin
  1 teaspoon dried thyme leaves
  ¼ teaspoon ground red pepper
  2 pounds boneless chicken breasts, cut
    into 1-inch pieces
    Vegetable oil
    Assorted mustards

In large bowl, combine onion soup mix, bread crumbs, chili powder, cumin, thyme and pepper. Dip chicken pieces in bread crumb mixture, coating well.

In large skillet, heat ½ inch oil over medium heat until hot. Cook chicken, stirring occasionally, until no longer pink in center; drain on paper towels. Serve warm with assorted mustards.

Makes about 5 dozen nuggets

Montmorency Cherry Chicken Salad

APPETIZERS & SALADS

GRILLED CHICKEN SALAD

¾ pound boneless skinless chicken breasts
½ teaspoon salt
½ teaspoon black pepper
1½ cups diagonally sliced zucchini
3 cups cooked rice, cooled to room temperature
1 can (14 ounces) artichoke hearts, drained
¾ cup fresh snow peas, blanched*
½ medium red bell pepper, cut into 1-inch cubes
⅓ cup light Italian salad dressing
1 teaspoon chopped fresh basil leaves
Lettuce leaves

*Substitute frozen snow peas, thawed, for fresh snow peas, if desired.

Season chicken with salt and black pepper. Grill or broil chicken until no longer pink in center. Place zucchini on grill during last 5 minutes of grilling or broiling. Cover and refrigerate chicken and zucchini until cold. Cut chicken into strips. Combine rice, chicken, zucchini, artichokes, snow peas and bell pepper in large bowl. Blend dressing and basil in small bowl. Pour over chicken mixture; toss lightly to coat. Serve on lettuce leaves.

Makes 4 servings

Favorite recipe from **USA Rice Council**

CHINATOWN STUFFED MUSHROOMS

24 large fresh mushrooms (about 1 pound)
½ pound ground turkey
1 clove garlic, minced
¼ cup fine dry bread crumbs
¼ cup thinly sliced green onions
3 tablespoons soy sauce, divided
1 teaspoon minced fresh ginger
1 egg white, slightly beaten
⅛ teaspoon crushed red pepper flakes (optional)

1. Remove stems from mushrooms; finely chop enough stems to equal 1 cup. Reserve remaining stems for use in salads, soups or stews, if desired.

2. Cook turkey with chopped stems and garlic in medium skillet over medium-high heat until turkey is no longer pink, stirring to separate turkey. Spoon off any fat.

3. Stir in bread crumbs, green onions, 2 tablespoons soy sauce, ginger, egg white and crushed red pepper; mix well.

4. Brush mushrooms lightly on all sides with remaining 1 tablespoon soy sauce; spoon about 2 teaspoons stuffing into each mushroom.* Place stuffed mushrooms on rack of foil-lined broiler pan. Broil 4 to 5 inches from heat 5 to 6 minutes until hot.   *Makes 8 servings (24 appetizers)*

*Mushrooms may be made ahead to this point; cover and refrigerate up to 24 hours. Add 1 to 2 minutes to broiling time for chilled mushrooms.

Grilled Chicken Salad

APPETIZERS & SALADS

RIO GRANDE QUESADILLAS

2 cups shredded cooked chicken
¾ cup water
1 package (1.25 ounces) LAWRY'S® Taco Spices & Seasonings
1 can (16 ounces) refried beans
6 large flour tortillas
1½ cups (6 ounces) shredded Monterey Jack cheese
¼ cup chopped pimiento
¼ cup chopped green onions
¼ cup chopped fresh cilantro
Vegetable oil
Salsa (optional)
Guacamole (optional)

In medium skillet, combine chicken, water and Taco Spices & Seasonings. Bring to a boil over medium-high heat; reduce heat and simmer, uncovered, 15 minutes. Stir in refried beans. Spread approximately ⅓ cup of chicken-bean mixture over half of each tortilla. Layer cheese, pimiento, green onions and cilantro evenly over chicken-bean mixture. Fold each tortilla in half. In large skillet, heat a small amount of oil over medium-high heat until hot. Quickly fry each quesadilla until slightly crisp, turning once.

Makes 6 servings

Presentation: Cut each quesadilla into quarters; serve with salsa and guacamole, if desired.

TURKEY SALAD VINAIGRETTE

2 tablespoons white wine vinegar
1 tablespoon olive oil
2 teaspoons lime juice
½ teaspoon salt
¼ teaspoon ground ginger
¼ teaspoon black pepper
1 pound Fully-Cooked No-Salt Turkey Breast, cut into ¼-inch cubes
¼ cup minced red onion
1 jalapeño pepper, seeded and minced
4 red leaf lettuce leaves
Bagel chips (optional)

1. In medium bowl, whisk together vinegar, oil, lime juice, salt, ginger and black pepper. Stir in turkey, onion and jalapeño pepper. Cover; refrigerate several hours before serving.

2. To serve, line each salad plate with lettuce; top with turkey mixture. Serve with bagel chips, if desired.

Makes 4 servings

Favorite recipe from **National Turkey Federation**

Rio Grande Quesadillas

APPETIZERS & SALADS

MEXICAN–STYLE ALMOND CHICKEN SALAD

4 boneless skinless chicken breast halves, cooked

⅓ cup *plus* 2 teaspoons vegetable oil, divided

1 cup BLUE DIAMOND® Blanched Slivered Almonds

6 tablespoons lime juice

5 teaspoons ground cumin

3 cloves garlic, finely chopped

½ teaspoon salt

⅛ teaspoon ground red pepper

6 tablespoons mayonnaise

1 small red onion, chopped

2 oranges, peeled, seeded and chopped
Additional vegetable oil for frying

4 large flour tortillas
Lettuce leaves
Sliced avocado, peeled orange slices, red onion rings and additional BLUE DIAMOND® Blanched Slivered Almonds for garnish

Cut chicken into 1-inch cubes; reserve. In medium skillet, heat 2 teaspoons oil over medium heat until hot. Add 1 cup almonds. Cook and stir in hot oil until golden; reserve. In large bowl, combine lime juice, cumin, garlic, salt and ground red pepper. Stir in mayonnaise and remaining ⅓ cup oil. Add reserved chicken, chopped onion and reserved almonds. Gently fold in oranges.

Heat a small amount of additional oil in medium skillet over medium-high heat until hot. Fry tortillas, 1 at a time, in hot oil, turning once, until crisp, puffed and golden; drain and set aside. (Press ladle in center of each tortilla while frying to form indentation.) To serve, line each tortilla with lettuce leaves; fill indentation with chicken mixture. Garnish each serving with avocado slices, orange slices, onion rings and additional almonds.

Makes 4 servings

DRUMS OF HEAVEN

1 tablespoon KIKKOMAN® Soy Sauce
1 tablespoon dry sherry
18 chicken wing drumettes
⅓ cup KIKKOMAN® Teriyaki Baste & Glaze
1 large clove garlic, minced
2 teaspoons sesame seed, toasted

Preheat oven to 425°F. Combine soy sauce and sherry in large bowl; add drumettes. Toss until well coated. Arrange drumettes, in single layer, on large rack in shallow foil-lined baking pan. Bake 30 minutes. Meanwhile, combine teriyaki baste & glaze and garlic in small bowl; brush tops of drumettes with half of glaze. Turn pieces over; brush with remaining glaze. Bake 15 minutes longer or until browned and juices run clear; sprinkle with sesame seed. *Makes 6 servings*

TURKEY & RICE SALAD

1 cup Vinaigrette Dressing (recipe follows), divided
3 cups hot cooked rice
2 cups cubed cooked turkey or chicken
1 cup pineapple chunks
1 can (8 ounces) peach halves, drained and cut into chunks
⅔ cup chopped peanuts
½ cup raisins
Salt and pepper to taste
Lettuce leaves
⅔ cup plain yogurt

Prepare Vinaigrette Dressing. Combine hot rice and ½ cup Vinaigrette Dressing in large bowl; stir to coat. Cool. Stir in turkey, pineapple, peaches, peanuts, raisins, salt, pepper and 6 tablespoons Vinaigrette Dressing.

Arrange lettuce leaves on individual serving plates; top with rice mixture. Blend yogurt and remaining 2 tablespoons Vinaigrette Dressing; spoon mixture over rice mixture. *Makes 4 servings*

Vinaigrette Dressing
¾ cup olive oil or vegetable oil
3 tablespoons wine vinegar or tarragon vinegar
1 tablespoon chopped fresh *or* 1 teaspoon dried parsley, basil or tarragon leaves
1 clove garlic, minced (optional)
1 teaspoon Dijon-style mustard
Salt and pepper to taste

Combine oil, vinegar, parsley, garlic, mustard, salt and pepper in small jar with tight-fitting lid; shake until well blended. Refrigerate until ready to use. Shake again before using.

Makes about 1 cup

Variation: For Lemon Vinaigrette Dressing, substitute 3 tablespoons lemon juice for vinegar and omit mustard.

APPETIZERS & SALADS

SAVORY MEXICAN POTATO TART

- **3 medium russet potatoes (about 1 pound), peeled, cooked and mashed**
- **½ cup all-purpose flour**
- **¼ cup cornmeal**
- **4 tablespoons vegetable oil, divided**
- **½ teaspoon garlic salt**
- **½ teaspoon black pepper**
- **1 jar (8 ounces) mild taco sauce**
- **1 medium onion, chopped**
- **1 cup shredded cooked turkey or chicken**
- **1 cup (4 ounces) shredded Monterey Jack cheese**
- **1 small jalapeño pepper, seeded and minced***
- **2 tablespoons chopped fresh oregano leaves *or* 2 teaspoons dried oregano leaves**
- **Prepared guacamole**
- **Cilantro leaves (optional)**

*Chili peppers can sting and irritate the skin; wear rubber gloves when handling peppers and do not touch eyes. Wash your hands after handling chili peppers.

Preheat oven to 350°F. Combine warm mashed potatoes, flour, cornmeal, 3 tablespoons oil, garlic salt and black pepper in large bowl; mix into smooth dough. Dust hands with flour. Press potato mixture onto bottom and up side of ungreased 10-inch flan or tart pan with removable bottom. Combine taco sauce with onion in small bowl; spread evenly over potato mixture. Top with turkey, cheese and jalapeño pepper. Sprinkle with oregano and remaining 1 tablespoon oil.

Bake 30 minutes or until potato mixture is heated through. Cool tart slightly, about 10 minutes. Carefully loosen tart from rim of pan using table knife. Remove rim from pan. Remove potato tart from pan bottom; cut into wedges to serve. Serve with guacamole. Garnish with cilantro, if desired.

Makes 8 to 10 servings

SMOKED TURKEY & PEPPER PASTA SALAD

- **¾ cup MIRACLE WHIP® Salad Dressing**
- **1 tablespoon Dijon-style mustard**
- **½ teaspoon dried thyme leaves**
- **8 ounces fettucini, cooked and drained**
- **1 cup (8 ounces) diced LOUIS RICH® Smoked Boneless Turkey Breast**
- **¾ cup zucchini slices, cut into halves**
- **½ cup red bell pepper strips**
- **½ cup yellow bell pepper strips**
- **Salt and black pepper**

Combine salad dressing, mustard and thyme in large bowl until well blended. Add pasta, turkey and vegetables; mix lightly. Season with salt and black pepper to taste. Cover; refrigerate at least 1 hour before serving. Add additional salad dressing before serving, if desired.

Makes about 6 servings

Prep time: 15 minutes plus chilling

Savory Mexican Potato Tart

HOT CHINESE CHICKEN SALAD

  8 chicken thighs, skinned, boned and cut into bite-sized pieces
¼ cup cornstarch
¼ cup vegetable oil
  1 large ripe tomato, cut into pieces
  1 can (4 ounces) water chestnuts, drained and sliced
  1 can (4 ounces) mushrooms, drained
  1 cup coarsely chopped green onions
  1 cup diagonally sliced celery
¼ cup soy sauce
  1 teaspoon monosodium glutamate (optional)
⅛ teaspoon garlic powder
  2 cups finely shredded iceberg lettuce
    Orange slices (optional)
    Hot cooked rice

Coat chicken, 1 piece at a time, in cornstarch. Heat oil in wok or large skillet over medium-high heat. Add chicken; stir-fry about 3 minutes or until browned. Add tomato, water chestnuts, mushrooms, green onions, celery, soy sauce, monosodium glutamate, if desired, and garlic powder. Cover; simmer 5 minutes or until chicken is no longer pink in center. Place lettuce on large serving plate. Top with chicken mixture; garnish with orange slices, if desired. Serve immediately with rice. *Makes 4 servings*

Favorite recipe from **National Broiler Council**

HAWAIIAN CHICKEN STRIPS

½ cup mayonnaise
  1 tablespoon Dijon-style mustard
  1 tablespoon honey
  4 cups RICE CHEX® Brand Cereal, crushed to make 1⅔ cups
½ cup flaked coconut
  1 pound boneless skinless chicken breasts, cut into ½-inch-wide strips
    Metal skewers
    Cherry tomatoes
    Pineapple chunks
    Green bell pepper chunks

Preheat oven to 400°F. Combine mayonnaise, mustard and honey in shallow dish. Combine cereal and coconut in another shallow dish or large resealable plastic food storage bag. Coat chicken strips, a few at a time, in mayonnaise mixture, then in cereal mixture.* Thread chicken strips onto metal skewers; place either cherry tomato, pineapple chunk or bell pepper chunk on end of each skewer. Arrange on rack in shallow baking pan. Bake 15 to 20 minutes or until chicken strips are no longer pink in centers.

Makes 25 to 30 appetizers

*Chicken strips may be coated a day before serving. Cover; refrigerate until ready to bake. Cooking time may need to be increased.

Hot Chinese Chicken Salad

CHICKEN POTATO SALAD OLÉ

2 large ripe tomatoes, seeded and chopped
¾ cup chopped green onions
¼ cup chopped cilantro
1 to 2 tablespoons chopped, seeded and pickled jalapeño peppers
1½ teaspoons salt, divided
1 cup HELLMANN'S® or BEST FOODS® Real Mayonnaise or Light Reduced Calorie Mayonnaise Dressing
3 tablespoons lime juice
1 teaspoon chili powder
1 teaspoon ground cumin
2 pounds small red potatoes, cooked and sliced ¼ inch thick
2 cups shredded cooked chicken
1 large yellow or red bell pepper, diced
Lettuce leaves
Tortilla chips, lime slices, whole chili peppers and cilantro sprigs for garnish (optional)

In medium bowl, combine tomatoes, green onions, chopped cilantro, jalapeño peppers and 1 teaspoon salt; set aside. In large bowl, combine mayonnaise, lime juice, chili powder, cumin and remaining ½ teaspoon salt. Add potatoes, chicken, bell pepper and half the tomato mixture; toss to coat well. Cover; refrigerate at least 1 hour before serving. To serve, spoon salad onto lettuce-lined platter. Spoon remaining tomato mixture over salad. If desired, garnish with tortilla chips, lime slices, whole chili peppers and cilantro sprigs. *Makes 6 servings*

SMOKED TURKEY ROLL–UPS

2 packages (4 ounces each) herb-flavored soft spreadable cheese, divided
4 (8-inch) flour tortillas*
2 packages (6 ounces each) Smoked Turkey Breast Slices
2 green onions, sliced crosswise into quarters
Whole pickled red cherry peppers (optional)

*To keep flour tortillas soft while preparing the turkey rolls, cover with a slightly damp cloth.

1. Spread 1 package cheese evenly over 1 side of each tortilla. Layer turkey slices evenly over cheese, overlapping turkey slices slightly to cover tortilla. Spread remaining 1 package cheese evenly over turkey slices.

2. At 1 edge of each tortilla, place 2 pieces of green onion. Roll up tortillas, jelly-roll style. Place turkey roll-ups, seam side down, in large resealable plastic food storage bag; seal tightly, pressing out air. Refrigerate several hours or overnight.

3. To serve, cut each turkey roll-up crosswise into ½-inch-thick slices to form pinwheels. If desired, arrange pinwheels on serving plate and garnish with cherry peppers in center.

Makes 56 servings

Favorite recipe from **National Turkey Federation**

Chicken Potato Salad Olé

FRESH FRUITY CHICKEN SALAD

    Yogurt Dressing (recipe follows)
2 cups cubed cooked chicken
1 cup cantaloupe melon balls
1 cup honeydew melon cubes
½ cup chopped celery
⅓ cup cashews
¼ cup sliced green onions
    Lettuce leaves

Prepare Yogurt Dressing; set aside. Combine chicken, melons, celery, cashews and green onions in large bowl. Add Yogurt Dressing; mix lightly. Cover; refrigerate at least 1 hour before serving. Serve on lettuce leaves. *Makes 4 servings*

Yogurt Dressing
¼ cup plain yogurt
3 tablespoons mayonnaise
3 tablespoons fresh lime juice
¾ teaspoon ground coriander
½ teaspoon salt
    Dash pepper

Combine all ingredients in small bowl; mix well.
Makes about ½ cup

QUICK TURKEY APPETIZERS

6 (10-inch) flour tortillas
4 teaspoons olive oil
1 cup salsa
1 pound deli-sliced Smoked Turkey, cut into ¼-inch strips
1 medium tomato, chopped
2 tablespoons chopped cilantro
1½ tablespoons chopped pitted ripe olives
½ teaspoon crushed red pepper
1 cup (4 ounces) shredded Monterey Jack cheese

1. Preheat oven to 400°F. Place tortillas on 2 baking sheets. Lightly brush both sides of tortillas with oil. Bake tortillas 3 minutes or until toasted, turning halfway through baking time; remove from oven.

2. Evenly spread salsa on each tortilla to within ½ inch of edge. Sprinkle turkey, tomato, cilantro, olives, red pepper and cheese evenly over salsa. Return to oven; bake 10 to 12 minutes or until cheese melts.

3. To serve, slice each tortilla into eighths.
Makes 48 appetizers

*Favorite recipe from **National Turkey Federation***

Fresh Fruity Chicken Salad

PAELLA SALAD

Garlic Dressing (recipe follows)
2½ cups water
1 cup uncooked rice
1 teaspoon salt
¼ to ½ teaspoon powdered saffron
2 cups cubed cooked chicken
1 cup cooked cleaned medium shrimp
  (about 4 ounces)
1 cup diced cooked artichoke hearts
½ cup cooked peas
2 tablespoons chopped salami
2 tablespoons thinly sliced green onions
2 tablespoons chopped drained pimiento
1 tablespoon minced fresh parsley
  Lettuce or fresh spinach leaves
1 large tomato, seeded and cubed

1. Place water in 1-quart saucepan; heat to a boil. Stir in rice, salt and saffron. Reduce heat; cover and simmer 20 minutes. Remove from heat; let stand until water is absorbed, about 5 minutes. Refrigerate about 15 minutes.

2. Place rice, chicken, shrimp, artichoke hearts, peas, salami, onions, pimiento and parsley in large bowl; toss well. Pour Garlic Dressing over salad; toss lightly to coat. Cover; refrigerate at least 1 hour before serving.

3. Arrange lettuce on large serving platter or individual serving plates; top with salad mixture. Garnish with tomato.   *Makes 4 to 6 servings*

Garlic Dressing
  ¾ cup olive oil or vegetable oil
  ¼ cup white wine vinegar
  1 teaspoon salt
  ½ teaspoon pepper
  1 clove garlic, minced

Combine all ingredients in small jar with tight-fitting lid. Shake well before using. (Dressing can be refrigerated up to 2 weeks.)   *Makes 1 cup*

RANCH BUFFALO WINGS

  ½ cup butter or margarine, melted
  ¼ cup hot pepper sauce
  3 tablespoons vinegar
24 chicken wing drumettes
  1 package (1 ounce) HIDDEN VALLEY
    RANCH® Milk Recipe Original Ranch®
    salad dressing mix
  ½ teaspoon paprika
  1 cup prepared HIDDEN VALLEY RANCH®
    Original Ranch® salad dressing
  Celery sticks

Preheat oven to 350°F. In small bowl, whisk together butter, pepper sauce and vinegar. Dip drumettes in butter mixture; arrange in single layer in large baking pan. Sprinkle with 1 package salad dressing mix. Bake 30 to 40 minutes or until chicken is browned and juices run clear. Sprinkle with paprika. Serve with 1 cup prepared salad dressing and celery sticks.

Makes 6 to 8 servings

Ranch Buffalo Wings

LAGOON CHICKEN SALAD

1½ cups unsweetened apple juice
2 whole chicken breasts (about 1½ pounds)
3 cups cooled cooked rice (1 cup uncooked)
1½ cups seedless green grapes, halved
1 cup chopped unpeeled apple
¾ cup slivered almonds, divided
½ cup chopped celery
½ cup chopped water chestnuts
1 cup mayonnaise
½ teaspoon seasoned salt
¼ teaspoon ground cinnamon
Spinach leaves
Apple slices (optional)

Bring apple juice to a boil in deep saucepan over medium-high heat; add chicken. Cover; reduce heat. Simmer about 30 minutes or until chicken is no longer pink in center. Remove chicken from saucepan to cool; discard liquid. When chicken is cool enough to handle, carefully remove and discard skin and bones. Dice chicken; place in large bowl. Add rice, grapes, apple, $1/2$ cup almonds, celery and water chestnuts; toss well. Combine mayonnaise, seasoned salt and cinnamon in small bowl. Add mayonnaise mixture to chicken mixture; toss lightly. Cover; refrigerate at least 30 minutes before serving. Spoon chicken salad onto spinach-lined serving platter. Sprinkle with remaining $1/4$ cup almonds. Garnish with apple slices, if desired. *Makes 4 to 6 servings*

*Favorite recipe from **National Broiler Council***

EMPANADITAS

2 teaspoons butter or margarine
½ cup finely chopped onion
1 cup finely chopped cooked chicken
2 tablespoons canned diced green chilies
2 teaspoons capers, drained and coarsely chopped
¼ teaspoon salt
½ cup (2 ounces) shredded Monterey Jack cheese
Pastry for double-crust 9-inch pie
1 egg yolk mixed with 1 teaspoon water

Preheat oven to 375°F. Melt butter in medium skillet over medium heat. Add onion; cook until tender. Stir in chicken, chilies, capers and salt; cook 1 minute. Remove from heat and let cool; stir in cheese.

Roll out pastry, one half at a time, on floured surface to a thickness of about $1/8$ inch; cut into $2^{1}/_{2}$-inch circles. Place about 1 teaspoon filling on each circle. Fold dough over to make half circles; seal edges with fork. Prick tops; brush with egg mixture. Place on ungreased baking sheets about 1 inch apart. Bake 12 to 15 minutes or until golden brown. Serve warm.

Makes about 3 dozen appetizers

Lagoon Chicken Salad

SUEZ MEZZE

- **1 large whole boneless skinless chicken breast**
- **1½ slices white sandwich bread**
- **1 egg yolk**
- **1 tablespoon minced fresh parsley**
- **1 tablespoon grated onion**
- **½ teaspoon salt**
- **¼ teaspoon ground cumin**
- **¼ teaspoon ground black pepper**
- **⅛ teaspoon garlic powder**
- **⅛ teaspoon ground turmeric**
- **⅓ cup all-purpose flour**
- **Vegetable oil**

1. Cut chicken into 1-inch pieces. Place chicken and bread in food processor; process until chicken is finely ground. Place ground chicken mixture in medium bowl; mix in egg yolk, parsley, onion, salt, cumin, pepper, garlic powder and turmeric. Cover; refrigerate 30 minutes.

2. Shape mixture into balls using 1 rounded teaspoon chicken mixture to form each ball; roll each ball lightly in flour to coat.

3. Heat 1 inch oil in 2-quart saucepan over medium-high heat until oil reaches 350°F. Fry balls, 6 at a time, in hot oil 3 to 4 minutes or until golden, turning often. Drain on paper towels. Keep warm in 200°F oven, if desired, until ready to serve. *Makes about 20 appetizers*

COBB SALAD

- **4 boneless skinless chicken breast halves, cooked and cooled**
- **⅔ cup vegetable oil**
- **⅓ cup HEINZ® Distilled White or Apple Cider Vinegar**
- **2 teaspoons dried dill weed**
- **1½ teaspoons sugar**
- **1 clove garlic, minced**
- **½ teaspoon salt**
- **¼ teaspoon black pepper**
- **8 cups torn salad greens, chilled**
- **1 large tomato, diced**
- **¾ cup crumbled blue cheese**
- **1 medium green bell pepper, diced**
- **6 slices bacon, cooked, drained and crumbled**
- **1 hard-cooked egg, chopped**
- **1 small red onion, chopped**

Shred chicken into bite-size pieces. For dressing, in screw-top jar, combine oil, vinegar, dill, sugar, garlic, salt and black pepper; cover and shake vigorously. Pour ½ cup dressing over chicken; toss well to coat. Toss greens with remaining dressing. Line each of 4 large individual salad bowls with greens; mound chicken mixture on one side. Fill in rest of bowls with rows of tomato, cheese, bell pepper, bacon, egg and onion.

Makes 4 servings

Cobb Salad

Hearty

SOUPS & SANDWICHES

THE CALIFORNIAN

3 tablespoons reduced-fat cream cheese,
   softened
1 tablespoon chutney
4 slices pumpernickel bread
4 washed lettuce leaves
¾ pound thinly sliced chicken breast (from
   deli)
1⅓ cups alfalfa sprouts
1 medium mango, peeled and sliced
1 pear, cored and sliced
4 strawberries

1. Combine cream cheese and chutney in small bowl; spread about 1 tablespoon on each bread slice. Place 1 lettuce leaf on cream cheese mixture. Divide chicken evenly; place on lettuce.

2. Arrange alfalfa sprouts on chicken; arrange mango and pear slices on sprouts. Garnish each open-faced sandwich with a strawberry. *Makes 4 servings*

INDIAN SUMMER TURKEY SOUP

4 cups water
1 envelope LIPTON® Recipe Secrets® Noodle Soup Mix with Real Chicken Broth
½ pound cooked smoked or regular turkey breast, diced
1 small tomato, diced
½ cup diagonally cut (1-inch) asparagus pieces
½ cup whole kernel corn
¼ teaspoon fennel seeds, crushed (optional)

In large saucepan, bring water to a boil over medium-high heat. Stir in remaining ingredients. Return to a boil. Reduce heat to low; simmer, uncovered, stirring occasionally, 5 minutes or until asparagus is tender.

MICROWAVE DIRECTIONS: In 2-quart microwave-safe casserole, combine water and fennel. Microwave, covered, at HIGH (100% power) 10 minutes or until boiling. Stir in remaining ingredients. Microwave, covered, 7 minutes at HIGH or until asparagus is tender, stirring once. Let stand, covered, 2 minutes.

Makes 6 (1-cup) servings

NEW YORKER PITA SANDWICHES

¾ pound boneless skinless chicken breasts, cut into ¼-inch strips
½ cup chopped onion
½ cup green bell pepper strips
1 tablespoon vegetable oil
1 can (16 ounces) HEINZ® Vegetarian Beans in Tomato Sauce
2 tablespoons HEINZ® Horseradish Sauce
¼ teaspoon salt
Dash black pepper
4 pocket pita breads (5-inch diameter)
8 slices tomato
8 lettuce leaves

In large skillet over medium-high heat, cook and stir chicken, onion and bell pepper in oil until vegetables are tender-crisp and chicken is no longer pink in center. Stir in beans with sauce, horseradish sauce, salt and black pepper. Reduce heat; simmer 5 minutes to blend flavors. Cut pitas in half; tuck 1 tomato slice and 1 lettuce leaf into each half. Fill each with about ⅓ cup chicken-bean mixture.

Makes 4 servings

Indian Summer Turkey Soup

CAJUN–STYLE CHICKEN SOUP

1½ **pounds chicken thighs**
4 **cups canned chicken broth**
1 **can (8 ounces) tomato sauce**
1 **medium onion, chopped**
2 **ribs celery, sliced**
2 **cloves garlic, minced**
2 **bay leaves**
1 **to** 1½ **teaspoons salt**
½ **teaspoon ground cumin**
¼ **teaspoon paprika**
¼ **teaspoon ground black pepper**
¼ **teaspoon ground red pepper**
  Dash ground white pepper
1 **large green bell pepper, chopped**
⅓ **cup uncooked rice**
8 **ounces fresh or thawed frozen okra, cut into ½-inch slices**
  Hot pepper sauce
  Fresh oregano leaves (optional)

Place chicken, chicken broth, tomato sauce, onion, celery, garlic, bay leaves, salt, cumin, paprika, black pepper, red pepper and white pepper in 5-quart Dutch oven. Bring to a boil over high heat. Reduce heat to medium-low; simmer, uncovered, 1 hour or until chicken is no longer pink in center.

Remove foam from surface of soup by skimming off with large spoon. Remove chicken from soup; let cool slightly. Remove fat from surface of soup by skimming off with large spoon.

Remove chicken meat from bones; discard skin and bones. Cut chicken into bite-sized pieces. Add chicken, bell pepper and rice to soup. Bring to a boil over high heat. Reduce heat to medium-low; simmer, uncovered, about 12 minutes or until rice is tender.

Add okra; simmer an additional 8 minutes or until okra is tender. Discard bay leaves. Ladle soup into bowls; serve with hot pepper sauce. Garnish with oregano, if desired. *Makes 6 servings*

Cajun–Style Chicken Soup

SOUPS & SANDWICHES

CHICKEN CHEESEBURGERS

3 cups ground chicken
2 eggs, slightly beaten
1 small onion, finely chopped
2 tablespoons dry bread crumbs
2 tablespoons minced fresh parsley
1 tablespoon grated Parmesan cheese
1 teaspoon salt
¼ teaspoon baking soda
¼ teaspoon ground white pepper
¼ teaspoon dried oregano leaves
2 tablespoons butter or margarine
2 tablespoons vegetable oil
4 slices (1 ounce each) American or
   Cheddar cheese
4 hamburger buns, split
4 tablespoons mayonnaise
4 lettuce leaves
4 to 8 tomato slices

Combine chicken, eggs, onion, bread crumbs, parsley, Parmesan cheese, salt, baking soda, pepper and oregano in large bowl. Mix well. Shape mixture into 4 round patties.

In large skillet over medium-low heat, heat butter and oil until butter melts; add patties. Cook 4 to 5 minutes on each side or until golden and no longer pink in center. Place 1 slice cheese on top of each patty. Cover skillet; cook about 1 minute or until cheese melts.

Spread each bun with 1 tablespoon mayonnaise. Place lettuce leaf on bottom half of each bun; top with patty, 1 or 2 tomato slices and top half of bun. Serve immediately. *Makes 4 servings*

CHICKEN LUNCHEON SANDWICHES

1½ cups chopped cooked chicken
1 cup (4 ounces) shredded Wisconsin
   Cheddar cheese
½ cup finely chopped celery
¼ cup finely chopped green bell pepper
1 green onion, chopped
1 tablespoon chopped drained pimiento
½ cup mayonnaise
½ cup plain yogurt
   Salt and black pepper to taste
   Rolls or bread
   Lettuce leaves

Combine chicken, cheese, celery, bell pepper, onion and pimiento in large bowl. Add mayonnaise and yogurt; toss until well coated. Season with salt and black pepper. Refrigerate until ready to use. Serve on rolls with lettuce. Garnish as desired. *Makes about 4½ cups*

Favorite recipe from **Wisconsin Milk Marketing Board**

Chicken Luncheon Sandwich

SOUPS & SANDWICHES

HEARTY CHICKEN AND RICE SOUP

10 cups chicken broth
1 medium onion, chopped
1 cup sliced celery
1 cup sliced carrots
¼ cup snipped fresh parsley
½ teaspoon cracked black pepper
½ teaspoon dried thyme leaves
1 bay leaf
1½ cups cubed chicken (about ¾ pound)
2 cups cooked rice
2 tablespoons lime juice
Lime slices for garnish

Combine broth, onion, celery, carrots, parsley, pepper, thyme and bay leaf in Dutch oven. Bring to a boil; stir once or twice. Reduce heat and simmer, uncovered, 10 to 15 minutes. Add chicken; simmer, uncovered, 5 to 10 minutes or until chicken is no longer pink in center. Remove and discard bay leaf. Stir in rice and lime juice just before serving. Garnish with lime slices.

Makes 8 servings

*Favorite recipe from **USA Rice Council***

MONTE CRISTO SANDWICHES

8 slices white sandwich bread
4 slices (1 ounce each) Swiss cheese
4 slices (1 ounce each) cooked ham
1 large whole boneless skinless chicken breast, cooked and thinly sliced
¼ teaspoon ground nutmeg
Pinch salt
½ cup milk
2 eggs
1 tablespoon butter or margarine
1 cup plain yogurt (optional)
2 tablespoons strawberry preserves (optional)

Cover each of 4 slices bread with 1 slice cheese and 1 slice ham, trimming edges to fit. Arrange chicken slices evenly over ham; sprinkle with nutmeg and salt. Cover each with a remaining bread slice; cut each sandwich in half diagonally. Beat milk and eggs in shallow bowl. Dip sandwich halves into egg mixture, coating both sides. In large skillet over medium-high heat, melt butter. Place sandwiches in skillet; cook 3 to 5 minutes on each side or until golden and hot throughout. Combine yogurt and preserves in small bowl. Serve hot sandwiches with yogurt mixture for dipping, if desired.

Makes 4 servings

Hearty Chicken and Rice Soup

SOUPS & SANDWICHES

SOFT TURKEY TACOS

    8 (6-inch) corn tortillas*
1½ teaspoons vegetable oil
    1 pound ground turkey
    1 small onion, chopped
    1 teaspoon dried oregano leaves
       Salt and pepper
       Chopped tomatoes
       Shredded lettuce
       Salsa

*Substitute 8 (10-inch) flour tortillas for corn tortillas, if desired.

1. Wrap tortillas in foil. Place in cold oven; set temperature to 350°F.

2. Heat oil in large skillet over medium heat. Add turkey and onion; cook until turkey is no longer pink, stirring occasionally. Stir in oregano. Season with salt and pepper to taste. Keep warm.

3. For each taco, fill warm tortilla with turkey mixture; top with tomatoes, lettuce and salsa.

Makes 4 servings

NOTE: To warm tortillas in microwave oven, wrap loosely in damp paper towels. Microwave on HIGH (100% power) 2 minutes or until hot.

CHICKEN CILANTRO BISQUE

    6 ounces boneless skinless chicken
       breasts, cut into chunks
2½ cups low-sodium chicken broth
    ½ cup cilantro leaves
    ½ cup sliced green onions
    ¼ cup sliced celery
    1 large clove garlic, minced
    ½ teaspoon ground cumin
    ⅓ cup all-purpose flour
1½ cups (12-ounce can) *undiluted*
       CARNATION® Evaporated Skimmed Milk
    Pepper

In large saucepan, combine chicken, broth, cilantro, green onions, celery, garlic and cumin. Heat to a boil; reduce heat and simmer, covered, 15 minutes. Pour soup into blender container. Add flour. Cover and blend, starting at low speed, until smooth. Pour mixture back into saucepan. Cook over medium heat, stirring constantly, until mixture comes to a boil and thickens. Remove from heat. Gradually stir in milk. Reheat just to serving temperature. *Do not boil.* Season with pepper to taste. Garnish as desired.

Makes about 4 servings

Soft Turkey Tacos

SOUPS & SANDWICHES

ARIZONA TURKEY STEW

5 medium carrots, cut into thick slices
1 large onion, cut into ½-inch pieces
3 tablespoons olive oil or vegetable oil
1 pound sliced turkey breast, cut into 1-inch strips
1 teaspoon LAWRY'S® Garlic Powder with Parsley
3 tablespoons all-purpose flour
8 small red potatoes, cut into ½-inch cubes
1 package (10 ounces) frozen peas, thawed
8 ounces sliced fresh mushrooms
1 cup beef broth
1 can (8 ounces) tomato sauce
1 package (1.62 ounces) LAWRY'S® Spices & Seasonings for Chili

Preheat oven to 450°F. In large skillet over medium heat, cook and stir carrots and onion in oil until tender. Stir in turkey strips and Garlic Powder with Parsley; cook 3 minutes or until turkey is just browned. Stir in flour. Pour mixture into 3-quart casserole dish. Stir in remaining ingredients. Bake, covered, 40 to 45 minutes or until potatoes are tender and turkey is no longer pink in center. Let stand 5 minutes before serving.

Makes 8 to 10 servings

STOVE-TOP DIRECTIONS: Prepare as directed in Dutch oven. Bring mixture to a boil. Reduce heat; cover and simmer 40 to 45 minutes or until potatoes are tender and turkey is no longer pink in center. Let stand 5 minutes before serving.

HINT: Spoon dollops of prepared dumpling mix on top of casserole during last 15 minutes of baking.

PRESENTATION: Serve with crisp green salad.

ZUCCHINI CHICKEN SOUP

½ cup chopped onion
½ cup chopped carrot
1 clove garlic, minced
1 tablespoon butter or margarine
1 cup diced cooked chicken
1 can (16 ounces) DEL MONTE® Zucchini with Italian-Style Tomato Sauce
1 can (14½ ounces) chicken broth

In medium skillet over medium-high heat, cook and stir onion, carrot and garlic in butter about 5 minutes or until vegetables are tender-crisp. Add remaining ingredients. Heat through and serve.

Makes 5 cups

Prep time: 10 minutes
Cook time: 10 minutes

Arizona Turkey Stew

CHICKEN CHILI

1 tablespoon vegetable oil
1 pound ground chicken or turkey
1 medium onion, chopped
1 medium green bell pepper, chopped
2 fresh jalapeño peppers, chopped*
1 can (28 ounces) tomatoes, cut up, undrained
1 can (15½ ounces) kidney beans, drained
1 can (8 ounces) tomato sauce
1 tablespoon chili powder
1 teaspoon salt
1 teaspoon dried oregano leaves
1 teaspoon ground cumin
¼ teaspoon ground red pepper
½ cup (2 ounces) shredded Cheddar cheese

*Chili peppers can sting and irritate the skin; wear rubber gloves when handling peppers and do not touch eyes. Wash your hands after handling chili peppers.

Heat oil in 5-quart Dutch oven or large saucepan over medium-high heat. Cook chicken, onion and bell pepper until chicken is no longer pink and onion is crisp-tender, stirring frequently to break up chicken. Stir in jalapeño peppers, tomatoes with juice, beans, tomato sauce, chili powder, salt, oregano, cumin and red pepper. Bring to a boil over high heat. Reduce heat to medium-low; simmer, uncovered, 45 minutes to blend flavors. To serve, spoon into bowls and top with cheese.

Makes 6 servings

GRECIAN CHICKEN SALAD SANDWICHES

2 cups chopped cooked chicken
1 cup chopped seeded cucumber
1 cup chopped seeded tomato
⅓ cup sliced green onions
¼ cup REALEMON® Lemon Juice from Concentrate
¼ cup vegetable oil
1 teaspoon sugar
1 clove garlic, finely chopped
½ teaspoon salt
¼ teaspoon dried basil leaves
2 cups shredded lettuce
4 pita bread rounds, halved

In medium bowl, combine chicken, cucumber, tomato and onions. In screw-top jar or cruet, combine ReaLemon® brand, oil, sugar, garlic, salt and basil; shake well. Pour over chicken mixture; toss to coat. Cover; marinate in refrigerator 2 hours. Just before serving, toss with lettuce. Serve in pita breads. Refrigerate leftovers.

Makes 4 sandwiches

Chicken Chili

MONTEREY CHICKEN SANDWICHES

1 tablespoon vegetable oil
1 tablespoon butter
4 boneless skinless chicken breast halves (about 1 pound)
1 teaspoon dried thyme leaves
  Salt and pepper
1 large red onion, thinly sliced
4 kaiser rolls, split
  Radicchio or lettuce leaves
  Mango chutney (optional)
  Olives (optional)

1. Heat oil and butter in large skillet over medium heat. Add chicken; sprinkle with thyme. Cook 8 minutes or until browned on both sides and no longer pink in center, turning after 4 minutes. Season with salt and pepper. Remove from skillet; keep warm.

2. Add onion to skillet; cook and stir until tender.

3. Fill rolls with radicchio leaves, chicken and onion. Serve with mango chutney and olives, if desired. *Makes 4 sandwiches*

TURKEY MEATBALL SOUP

1 pound ground turkey
⅔ cup matzo meal
¼ cup EGG BEATERS® 99% Real Egg Product
2 tablespoons FLEISCHMANN'S® Sweet Unsalted Spread
2 cloves garlic, minced
6 cups water
4 cups low-sodium tomato juice
1½ cups uncooked tri-color pasta twists
2 large carrots, peeled and thinly sliced
2 large tomatoes, chopped
1 large onion, chopped
1 tablespoon Italian seasoning
½ teaspoon ground black pepper
1 (10-ounce) package frozen chopped spinach, thawed

In small bowl, thoroughly mix turkey, matzo meal and egg product. Shape into 24 (1-inch) meatballs. In large saucepan over medium-high heat, brown meatballs, in batches, in spread. Remove meatballs. In same saucepan, cook and stir garlic for 3 minutes or until lightly browned. Add water, tomato juice, meatballs, pasta, carrots, tomatoes, onion, Italian seasoning and pepper. Heat to a boil. Cover; reduce heat. Simmer 15 minutes. Add spinach; cook an additional 5 minutes or until pasta is tender. *Makes 10 (1½-cup) servings*

Monterey Chicken Sandwich

SOUPS & SANDWICHES

CHICKEN KABOBS IN PITA BREAD

¼ cup olive oil or vegetable oil
¼ cup lemon juice
½ teaspoon salt
½ teaspoon dried oregano leaves
¼ teaspoon garlic powder
⅛ teaspoon ground black pepper
1 whole boneless skinless chicken breast, cut into 1-inch cubes
4 small metal skewers
2 large pita breads
1 small onion, thinly sliced
1 tomato, thinly sliced
½ cup plain yogurt
Chopped fresh parsley (optional)

1. Combine oil, lemon juice, salt, oregano, garlic powder and pepper in medium glass bowl. Add chicken; toss until well coated. Cover; marinate in refrigerator at least 3 hours or overnight.

2. Remove chicken from marinade, reserving marinade. Thread chicken onto skewers. Place kabobs on greased broiler pan. Broil about 5 inches from heat until chicken is golden, 8 to 10 minutes, brushing often with marinade. Turn kabobs over and brush with marinade. Broil until chicken is no longer pink in center, 5 to 7 minutes. Discard any remaining marinade.

3. Cut each pita bread in half; gently pull each half open to form a pocket. Remove chicken from 1 kabob and place inside 1 pocket; repeat with remaining kabobs. Top with onion, tomato and yogurt. Garnish with parsley, if desired. Serve hot.

Makes 4 servings

TROPICAL TURKEY MELT

1 English muffin, split
1 teaspoon Dijon-style mustard
3 ounces smoked turkey slices
3 thin slices papaya
1 slice Monterey Jack cheese
Butter or margarine, softened

Spread inside of muffin halves with mustard. On 1 half, layer turkey, papaya and cheese. Press remaining muffin half, mustard side down, over cheese. Spread butter on outside of muffin halves. Cook sandwich in small skillet over medium heat until toasted, about 4 minutes; turn and cook on remaining side until toasted and cheese is melted. Serve hot. Garnish as desired. *Makes 1 serving*

Tropical Turkey Melt

SOUPS & SANDWICHES

CHICKEN SOUP PARMIGIANA

3 cups water
1 envelope LIPTON® Recipe Secrets® Noodle Soup Mix with Real Chicken Broth
1 cup chopped fresh tomatoes *or* 1 can (8 ounces) whole peeled tomatoes, undrained and chopped
½ pound boneless chicken breasts, cut into ½-inch pieces
½ teaspoon dried oregano leaves
½ teaspoon garlic powder
½ teaspoon dried basil leaves*
1 cup sliced zucchini or yellow squash
⅓ cup (about 1 ounce) shredded mozzarella cheese
Grated Parmesan cheese (optional)

*SUBSTITUTION: Use 2 teaspoons chopped fresh basil leaves.

MICROWAVE DIRECTIONS: In 2-quart microwave-safe casserole, combine all ingredients except zucchini and cheeses; stir well. Microwave at HIGH (100% power) 5 minutes, stirring once. Stir in zucchini. Microwave, uncovered, at HIGH 11 minutes or until chicken is no longer pink in center; stir. To serve, spoon into bowls; sprinkle with mozzarella and, if desired, Parmesan cheese.
Makes about 5 cups

CONVENTIONAL DIRECTIONS: In medium saucepan, combine all ingredients except cheeses. Bring to a boil. Reduce heat; simmer, stirring occasionally, 5 minutes or until chicken is no longer pink in center. Serve as above.

CHICKEN CORN CHOWDER

1½ cups cubed cooked chicken or turkey
4 slices bacon
½ cup chopped onion
½ teaspoon dried thyme leaves
3 tablespoons flour
3 cups BORDEN® or MEADOW GOLD® Half-and-Half *or* Milk
2 cups water
1 (10-ounce) package frozen whole kernel corn
1 medium potato, peeled and diced
2 tablespoons WYLER'S® or STEERO® Chicken-Flavor Instant Bouillon *or* 6 Chicken-Flavor Bouillon Cubes
¼ teaspoon pepper

In large saucepan, cook bacon until crisp; remove and crumble. In drippings, cook and stir onion and thyme until onion is tender; stir in flour until smooth. Add chicken and remaining ingredients except bacon; bring to a boil. Reduce heat; simmer 30 minutes or until vegetables are tender, stirring occasionally. Garnish with bacon. Refrigerate leftovers.
Makes about 1¾ quarts

TIP: Two (5- or 6¾-ounce) cans chunk chicken may be substituted for cooked chicken; add during last 10 minutes of cooking time.

Chicken Soup Parmigiana

CHICKEN NOODLE SOUP

5 (14½-ounce) cans ready-to-serve chicken broth
2 cups water
1 small onion, cut into small wedges
1 cup sliced carrots
1 cup sliced celery (including leaves)
2 tablespoons WYLER'S® or STEERO® Chicken-Flavor Instant Bouillon
1 teaspoon dried parsley flakes
1 teaspoon dried basil leaves
¼ teaspoon pepper
½ (1-pound) package CREAMETTE® Egg Noodles, uncooked
2 cups chopped cooked chicken

In Dutch oven, combine broth, water, onion, carrots, celery, bouillon, parsley, basil and pepper. Bring to a boil. Reduce heat; simmer 15 minutes. Prepare noodles according to package directions; drain. Add egg noodles and chicken to soup; heat through. Garnish as desired. Refrigerate leftovers.

Makes about 4 quarts

PARTY HERO

¾ pound creamy coleslaw
⅓ cup bottled salad dressing (Thousand Island, creamy Italian or creamy blue cheese), divided
1 (8-inch) round loaf of bread (French, Italian, rye or sourdough), about 1½ pounds
Leaf lettuce
½ pound cooked turkey, thinly sliced
½ pound cooked ham, thinly sliced
¼ pound Cheddar, Muenster or Swiss cheese, sliced

Drain excess liquid from coleslaw; add 2 tablespoons bottled dressing to coleslaw, mixing well. Cut a thin slice from top of bread; spread cut surface of slice with some of the bottled dressing. Hollow out bread, leaving about ¹/₂-inch-thick bread shell. Line bread shell with some of lettuce; brush with remaining bottled dressing. Press turkey onto bottom; cover with half of coleslaw mixture. Top with ham, remaining coleslaw mixture and cheese. Top with lettuce; cover with top bread slice. Place 6 to 8 long wooden toothpicks into sandwich to secure. Refrigerate no longer than 4 to 6 hours before serving. To serve, cut between toothpicks to form 6 to 8 wedge-shaped sandwiches. *Makes 6 to 8 servings*

SOUPS & SANDWICHES

BRUNSWICK STEW

- **1 stewing chicken (about 4½ pounds), cut into serving pieces**
- **2 quarts water**
- **1 stalk celery (including leaves), cut into 2-inch pieces**
- **1 small onion, quartered**
- **2 teaspoons salt**
- **1 teaspoon whole peppercorns**
- **1 small clove garlic, halved**
- **1 can (16 ounces) tomatoes, cut into 1-inch pieces, undrained**
- **2 medium potatoes, peeled and cubed**
- **1 onion, thinly sliced**
- **¼ cup tomato paste**
- **1 teaspoon sugar**
- **½ teaspoon ground black pepper**
- **½ teaspoon dried thyme leaves**
- **⅛ teaspoon garlic powder**
- **Dash hot pepper sauce**
- **1 package (10 ounces) frozen lima beans**
- **1 package (10 ounces) frozen whole kernel corn**

1. Place chicken, giblets and neck in 5-quart Dutch oven; add water. Heat to a boil; skim off foam. Add celery, quartered onion, salt, peppercorns and garlic; heat to a boil. Reduce heat; cover and simmer until thighs are no longer pink in center, 2½ to 3 hours.

2. Remove chicken pieces from broth; cool slightly. Remove meat from bones, discarding bones and skin. Chop enough chicken into 1-inch pieces to measure 3 cups; set aside. Reserve remaining chicken for another use.

3. Skim fat from chicken broth. Strain broth through fine strainer, discarding vegetables, giblets and peppercorns. Return 1 quart broth to Dutch oven. Reserve remaining broth for another use.

4. Add tomatoes with juice, potatoes, sliced onion, tomato paste, sugar, ground black pepper, thyme, garlic powder and hot pepper sauce. Heat to a boil. Reduce heat; cover and simmer 30 minutes.

5. Add beans and corn to stew. Heat to a boil. Reduce heat; cover and simmer 5 minutes. Add chopped chicken; simmer 5 minutes longer. Serve hot. *Makes 6 to 8 servings*

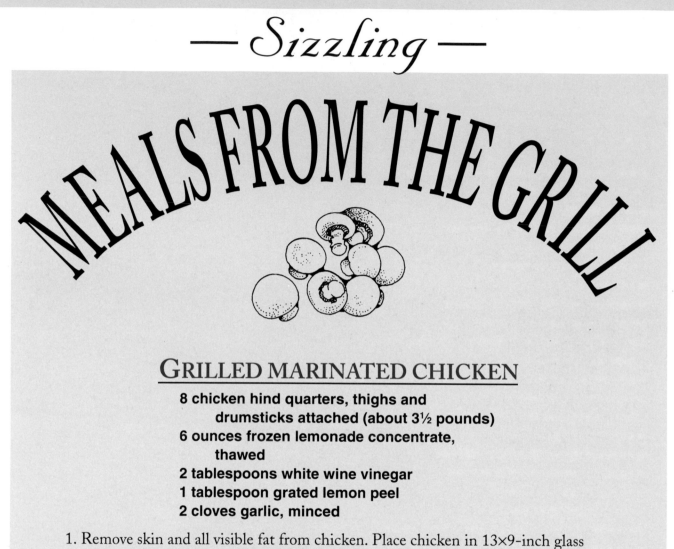

Sizzling

MEALS FROM THE GRILL

GRILLED MARINATED CHICKEN

**8 chicken hind quarters, thighs and
   drumsticks attached (about 3½ pounds)
6 ounces frozen lemonade concentrate,
   thawed
2 tablespoons white wine vinegar
1 tablespoon grated lemon peel
2 cloves garlic, minced**

1. Remove skin and all visible fat from chicken. Place chicken in 13×9-inch glass baking dish. Combine remaining ingredients in small bowl; blend well. Pour over chicken; turn to coat. Cover; refrigerate 3 hours or overnight, turning occasionally.

2. To prevent sticking, spray grid with nonstick cooking spray. Prepare coals for grilling.

3. Place chicken on grill 4 inches from medium-hot coals. Grill 20 to 30 minutes or until chicken is no longer pink near bone, turning occasionally. (Do not overcook or chicken will be dry.) Garnish with curly endive and lemon peel strips, if desired.

Makes 8 servings

SPICY LIME AND CILANTRO TURKEY FAJITAS

1 pound Turkey Tenderloins
1 tablespoon paprika
½ teaspoon onion salt
½ teaspoon garlic powder
½ teaspoon ground red pepper
½ teaspoon fennel seeds
½ teaspoon dried thyme leaves
¼ teaspoon white pepper
Sour Cream Sauce (recipe follows)
1 lime, halved
4 pita breads
Shredded lettuce (optional)

1. Slice tenderloins open lengthwise, cutting almost through, being careful to leave halves attached. Open halves flat. In shallow dish, combine paprika, onion salt, garlic powder, ground red pepper, fennel seeds, thyme and white pepper. Rub mixture over tenderloins; cover and refrigerate 1 hour. Prepare Sour Cream Sauce.

2. Prepare grill for direct cooking. Grill tenderloins, on covered grill, 10 to 12 minutes or until meat thermometer inserted into thickest part of tenderloin registers 170°F, turning halfway through grilling time. Place on clean serving plate; squeeze lime over tenderloins. Cut tenderloins crosswise into ¹/₄-inch-thick slices.

3. To serve, top each pita with tenderloins and Sour Cream Sauce; roll up. Garnish with lettuce, if desired.

Sour Cream Sauce

1 cup fat-free imitation sour cream
¼ cup thinly sliced green onions
¼ cup finely chopped cilantro
1 can (4 ounces) chopped green chilies, drained
1 plum tomato, seeded and finely chopped
½ teaspoon black pepper
¼ teaspoon ground red pepper

In small bowl, combine sour cream, onions, cilantro, chilies, tomato and black and ground red peppers. Cover; refrigerate until ready to use.

Favorite recipe from **National Turkey Federation**

CAJUN CHICKEN BURGERS

1 pound fresh ground chicken
1 small onion, finely chopped
¼ cup chopped green or red bell pepper
3 green onions, minced
1 clove garlic, minced
1 teaspoon Worcestershire sauce
½ teaspoon TABASCO® pepper sauce
Ground black pepper

In medium bowl, combine chicken, chopped onion, bell pepper, green onions, garlic, Worcestershire sauce, Tabasco® sauce and black pepper. Form into 5 (3-inch-diameter) patties. Broil or grill 6 minutes; turn over and broil or grill an additional 4 to 6 minutes or until no longer pink in centers. Serve immediately.

Makes 5 servings

Spicy Lime and Cilantro Turkey Fajitas

MEALS FROM THE GRILL

TURKEY SATAY WITH PEANUT SAUCE

1 pound Turkey Tenderloins
3 tablespoons skim milk
1 tablespoon dried onion flakes
1 tablespoon olive oil
1 teaspoon reduced-sodium soy sauce
½ teaspoon crushed red pepper
½ teaspoon grated lemon peel
¼ teaspoon ground ginger
⅛ teaspoon coconut extract
Nonstick cooking spray
Bamboo skewers
Peanut Sauce (recipe follows)

1. Cut turkey tenderloins in half lengthwise. Place between 2 pieces waxed paper. Pound with meat mallet to flatten. Cut lengthwise into 1-inch-wide strips.

2. In resealable plastic food storage bag, combine milk, onion flakes, oil, soy sauce, red pepper, lemon peel, ginger and coconut extract. Add turkey strips. Seal bag tightly, turning to coat strips. Marinate in refrigerator at least 4 hours.

3. Remove grill rack from charcoal grill; lightly coat with nonstick cooking spray. Set aside. Prepare grill for direct cooking.

4. Meanwhile, soak bamboo skewers in water 15 minutes; drain. Drain marinade from bag; discard. Weave turkey strips onto skewers. Position grill rack over hot coals. Grill turkey, on covered grill, 4

to 6 minutes or until turkey is no longer pink in center, turning halfway through grilling time. Serve with Peanut Sauce. Garnish as desired.

Makes 8 servings

Peanut Sauce
1 tablespoon coarsely chopped onion
1 small clove garlic
¼ cup creamy peanut butter
1½ teaspoons lemon juice
¼ teaspoon reduced-sodium soy sauce
⅛ teaspoon ground red pepper
Dash coconut extract
¼ cup skim milk

MICROWAVE DIRECTIONS: Process onion and garlic in food processor until finely chopped. Add peanut butter, lemon juice, soy sauce, ground red pepper and coconut extract. Process until blended. With motor running, slowly add milk through feed tube. Process until sauce is smooth and well blended, stopping motor to scrape sides often.

Pour sauce into 1-cup glass measure. Microwave at HIGH (100% power) 20 to 30 seconds or until slightly thickened.

Favorite recipe from **National Turkey Federation**

Turkey Satay with Peanut Sauce

MEALS FROM THE GRILL

APRICOT–STUFFED CHICKEN

½ **cup stuffing mix**
¼ **cup chopped green onions**
2 **tablespoons butter, melted**
½ **teaspoon ground ginger, divided**
2 **whole chicken breasts, boned**
4 **fresh California apricots, halved and pitted (about ½ pound)**
½ **cup apricot jam**
1 **tablespoon cider vinegar**

In small bowl, combine stuffing mix, onions, butter and ¼ teaspoon ginger. Place chicken, skin side down, on tray or cutting board. Pound with flat side of meat mallet or rolling pin to flatten slightly. Spoon half of stuffing mixture in lengthwise strip along center of each breast. Place apricot halves on top of stuffing mixture. Roll up chicken lengthwise, jelly-roll style. Tie each chicken roll with string every two inches.

Prepare grill for direct cooking. Grill chicken, on covered grill, over medium-hot coals 15 minutes, turning once or twice. Combine apricot jam, vinegar and remaining ¼ teaspoon ginger in small bowl. Brush apricot mixture over chicken rolls; continue grilling 5 to 10 minutes or until chicken is no longer pink in center. *Makes 4 servings*

Favorite recipe from **California Apricot Advisory Board**

ZESTY GRILLED CALIFORNIA TURKEY WINGS

3 **cans beer** *or* 4 **cups chicken broth**
1 **teaspoon salt**
½ **teaspoon pepper**
4 **California-grown turkey wings**
1 **can (16 ounces) Italian-style tomatoes, drained**
½ **cup** *each* **chopped onion, cider vinegar, melted butter**
2 **tablespoons** *each* **firmly packed brown sugar, Worcestershire sauce**
½ **teaspoon** *each* **curry powder, chili powder**

Combine beer, salt and pepper in large saucepan. Bring to a boil over medium-high heat. Add turkey wings. Reduce heat; simmer 30 minutes. Remove turkey wings; reserve ½ cup beer broth. Place tomatoes, onion, vinegar, reserved beer broth, butter, brown sugar, Worcestershire sauce, curry powder and chili powder in blender or food processor; blend or process until smooth. Pour mixture into medium saucepan. Cook sauce over medium heat 20 minutes or until sauce boils and is slightly thickened. Reserve half of sauce for basting. Prepare charcoal grill for direct cooking. Grill wings, on covered grill, 30 minutes or until browned and juices run clear, basting frequently with reserved sauce. Serve wings with remaining sauce. *Makes 4 servings*

Favorite recipe from **California Poultry Industry Federation**

Apricot-Stuffed Chicken

MEALS FROM THE GRILL

SOY–HONEY GRILLED TURKEY TENDERLOINS

1 pound Turkey Tenderloins
2 tablespoons reduced-sodium soy sauce
1 tablespoon dry sherry
1 tablespoon honey
1 teaspoon toasted sesame seeds
½ teaspoon sesame seed oil
1 small garlic clove, minced

1. Slice turkey tenderloins open lengthwise, cutting almost through, being careful to leave 2 halves attached. Open halves flat.

2. In large shallow glass dish, combine soy sauce, sherry, honey, sesame seeds, oil and garlic. Place tenderloins in mixture, turning to coat thoroughly. Cover; marinate in refrigerator 20 minutes.

3. Prepare grill for direct cooking. Drain tenderloins; discard marinade. Grill tenderloins, on covered grill, 10 to 12 minutes or until meat thermometer inserted into thickest part of tenderloin registers 170°F, turning halfway through grilling time.   *Makes 4 servings*

*Favorite recipe from **National Turkey Federation***

TURKEY CARIBE

8 LOUIS RICH® Fresh Turkey Breast Slices
** (about 1 pound)**
4 slices American cheese
¼ teaspoon garlic powder
¼ teaspoon onion powder
¼ teaspoon dried oregano leaves
8 slices bacon

Top each of 4 turkey slices with 1 slice cheese folded in half. Combine garlic powder, onion powder and oregano in small bowl; sprinkle evenly over each piece of cheese. Top with remaining turkey slices. Wrap each turkey bundle crosswise with 2 slices bacon, securing with toothpicks. Grill turkey bundles, on covered grill, 6 inches from medium-hot coals 15 minutes or until turkey is no longer pink in center, turning frequently. Remove toothpicks before serving.   *Makes 4 servings*

Turkey Caribe

CHINESE KABOBS

    2 tablespoons reduced-sodium soy sauce
    2 green onions, thinly sliced
    2 teaspoons red wine vinegar
    ½ teaspoon ground ginger
    ½ teaspoon Chinese five-spice powder
    1 pound Turkey Tenderloins, cut into 1-inch
        cubes
      Nonstick cooking spray
      Bamboo skewers
      Plum Sauce (recipe follows)

1. In large resealable plastic food storage bag, combine soy sauce, green onions, vinegar, ginger and five-spice powder. Add turkey. Seal bag tightly, turning to coat turkey. Marinate in refrigerator at least 4 hours.

2. Remove grill rack from charcoal grill; lightly coat with nonstick cooking spray. Set aside. Prepare grill for direct cooking.

3. Soak bamboo skewers in water 15 minutes; drain. Drain marinade from bag; discard. Thread turkey cubes onto skewers. Position grill rack over hot coals. Grill turkey, on covered grill, 10 to 12 minutes or until turkey is no longer pink in center, turning halfway through grilling time. Serve with Plum Sauce.   *Makes 8 servings*

Plum Sauce
    ½ cup plum preserves
    3 tablespoons red wine vinegar
    1½ teaspoons dried onion flakes
    1 teaspoon reduced-sodium chicken
        bouillon granules
    1 teaspoon reduced-sodium soy sauce
    ½ teaspoon ground ginger
    ½ teaspoon Chinese five-spice powder

MICROWAVE DIRECTIONS: Combine preserves, vinegar, onion flakes, bouillon granules, soy sauce, ginger and five-spice powder in 2-cup glass measure. Microwave at HIGH (100% power) 4 to 5 minutes, stirring every minute or until sauce is slightly thickened.

*Favorite recipe from **National Turkey Federation***

ALL–AMERICAN BARBECUED ROASTER

1 PERDUE® Oven Stuffer Roaster (5 to 7 pounds)
Salt
Pepper
1 cup vegetable oil
⅓ cup red wine vinegar
1 teaspoon paprika

Preheat gas grill following manufacturer's directions. Or, prepare charcoal grill for indirect cooking, arranging coals on each side of rectangular metal or foil drip pan. Add mesquite or hickory chunks or chips, if desired, for additional smoky flavor.

Remove giblets from roaster; reserve for other uses. Rinse roaster under cold running water; pat dry with paper towels. Sprinkle salt and pepper inside cavity and over outside of roaster, if desired. Tuck wings under back; tie legs together with wet kitchen string.

To prepare basting sauce, in small bowl, combine oil, vinegar, paprika, 2 teaspoons salt and ½ teaspoon pepper; whisk until well combined and thickened. Place roaster, breast side up, on grid directly over drip pan. Grill roaster, on covered grill, 30 minutes; turn and brush with basting sauce. Continue to grill, covered, 15 minutes per pound, brushing with basting sauce every 15

minutes until legs move freely and juices run clear. If necessary, wrap small pieces of foil around wings and drumsticks to prevent burning. Bring any leftover basting sauce to a boil and serve with roaster. *Makes 6 servings*

INTERNATIONAL BASTING SAUCE VARIATIONS

Italian Roaster: Prepare basting sauce as directed, adding 1 cup ketchup, 2 cloves minced garlic, 1 teaspoon dried oregano leaves and ½ teaspoon dried basil leaves to sauce.

French Roaster: Prepare basting sauce as directed, adding ⅓ cup minced shallots, ⅓ cup Dijon-style mustard and 1 teaspoon dried tarragon leaves to sauce.

German Roaster: Prepare basting sauce as directed, adding ½ cup beer, 2 tablespoons molasses and 2 tablespoons caraway seeds to sauce.

Chinese Roaster: Prepare basting sauce as directed, adding ⅓ cup soy sauce, 2 cloves minced garlic and 1 tablespoon grated fresh ginger or 1 teaspoon ground ginger to sauce.

MEALS FROM THE GRILL

BARBECUED CHICKEN WITH CHILI–ORANGE GLAZE

   1 to 2 dried de árbol chilies*
1½ teaspoons shredded orange peel
   ½ cup fresh orange juice
   2 tablespoons tequila
   2 cloves garlic, minced
   ¼ teaspoon salt
   ¼ cup vegetable oil
   1 broiler-fryer chicken (about 3 pounds), cut
      into quarters
      Orange slices (optional)
      Cilantro sprigs (optional)

*For milder flavor, discard seeds from chili peppers. Since chili peppers can sting and irritate the skin, wear rubber gloves when handling peppers and do not touch eyes. Wash your hands after handling chili peppers.

Crush chilies into coarse flakes in mortar with pestle. Combine chilies, orange peel, orange juice, tequila, garlic and salt in small bowl. Gradually add oil, whisking continuously, until marinade is thoroughly blended.

Arrange chicken in single layer in shallow glass baking dish. Pour marinade over chicken; turn pieces to coat. Marinate, covered, in refrigerator 2 to 3 hours, turning chicken over and basting with marinade several times.

Prepare charcoal grill for direct cooking or preheat broiler. Drain chicken, reserving marinade. Bring marinade to a boil in small saucepan over high heat. Grill chicken on covered grill or broil, 6 to 8 inches from heat, for 15 minutes, brushing frequently with marinade. Turn chicken over. Grill or broil 15 minutes more or until chicken is no longer pink in center and juices run clear, brushing frequently with marinade. Garnish with orange slices and cilantro, if desired.   *Makes 4 servings*

ISLAND GRILLED TURKEY BREAST

   1 (4- to 5-pound) fresh turkey breast half
Sauce:
   ¼ cup butter, melted
   ⅓ cup honey
   1 tablespoon Dijon-style mustard
   1 teaspoon curry powder
   ¼ teaspoon garlic powder

Rinse turkey under cold water; pat dry with paper towels. Prepare grill for indirect cooking, arranging coals on both sides of rectangular metal or foil drip pan. Place turkey on rack over drip pan. Grill turkey, on covered grill, over hot coals 2 to 2½ hours or until meat thermometer inserted in thickest part registers 170°F and turkey is no longer pink in center. (Add additional coals during grilling, if necessary, to maintain hot coals.) Meanwhile, combine sauce ingredients in small bowl. Brush turkey with sauce frequently during last 30 minutes of grilling. Let stand 10 minutes before slicing.
      Makes 8 to 10 servings

Barbecued Chicken with Chili-Orange Glaze

CARIBBEAN LEMON CHICKEN

1 (3- to 3½-pound) frying chicken, quartered
½ cup KIKKOMAN® Teriyaki Sauce
1 teaspoon grated lemon peel
1 tablespoon lemon juice
2 teaspoons TABASCO® pepper sauce
¼ teaspoon ground cinnamon

Place chicken in large resealable plastic food storage bag. Combine teriyaki sauce, lemon peel, lemon juice, Tabasco® sauce and cinnamon in small bowl; pour over chicken. Press air out of bag; seal top securely. Turn bag several times to coat chicken well. Marinate in refrigerator 8 hours or overnight, turning bag occasionally. Drain chicken; discard marinade. Broil chicken 5 to 7 inches from heat source or grill chicken over hot coals 40 to 50 minutes or until juices run clear, turning chicken occasionally during cooking.   *Makes 4 servings*

ALL–AMERICAN TURKEY BURGERS

1 pound Ground Turkey
½ cup chopped onion
¼ cup ketchup
1 clove garlic, minced
⅛ teaspoon pepper
4 kaiser rolls, split
4 leaves lettuce
4 slices tomato
4 slices onion

1. Prepare charcoal grill for direct cooking.

2. In medium bowl, combine turkey, onion, ketchup, garlic and pepper. Shape turkey mixture into 4 burgers, approximately 3½ inches in diameter.

3. Grill burgers, on covered grill, 10 to 12 minutes for medium or until desired doneness is reached, turning halfway through grilling time.

4. To serve, place each burger on bottom half of roll; top with lettuce, tomato and onion. Add top half of roll.   *Makes 4 servings*

Favorite recipe from **National Turkey Federation**

TURKEY NORMANDE

**1 package (about 2 pounds) LOUIS RICH®
Fresh Turkey Drumsticks**

SAUCE:
1 cup apple butter
2 tablespoons soy sauce

Rinse turkey under cold water; pat dry with paper towels. Wrap each drumstick in heavy-duty foil. Grill turkey, on covered grill, over medium-hot coals 45 minutes. Turn; cook an additional 45 minutes, adding additional coals during grilling, if necessary, to maintain medium-hot coals. Meanwhile, combine sauce ingredients in small bowl. Remove turkey from foil. Brush with sauce; grill an additional 10 minutes or until turkey is no longer pink in center, turning occasionally. Boil remaining sauce in small saucepan; serve with turkey. *Makes 2 servings*

TO MAKE AHEAD: Rinse turkey under cold water; pat dry with paper towels. Place in Dutch oven or large skillet with 1 cup water. Bring to a boil; reduce heat. Cover; simmer 2 hours. Pour off liquid. Cover and refrigerate. Prepare sauce as directed above. Grill turkey, on covered grill, over medium-hot coals 30 minutes, turning occasionally. Brush with sauce and grill an additional 10 minutes or until turkey is no longer pink in center, turning occasionally. Boil remaining sauce in small saucepan; serve with turkey.

BARBECUED GLAZED CHICKEN

1 jar (16 ounces) orange marmalade
⅓ cup soy sauce
¼ cup cider vinegar
2 cloves garlic, minced
1 broiler-fryer chicken (2 to 3 pounds), quartered
¼ cup vegetable oil
Salt and pepper

Combine orange marmalade, soy sauce, vinegar and garlic in small bowl; set aside. Brush all sides of chicken with oil; sprinkle with salt and pepper. Lightly oil grid. Grill chicken, skin side up, on uncovered grill, over medium-hot KINGSFORD® briquets about 45 minutes, turning often, until juices run clear. During last 20 minutes of grilling, brush chicken with marmalade sauce.

Makes 4 servings

— *Terrific* —
SUPPERTIME DISHES

HONEY LIME GLAZED CHICKEN

1 broiler-fryer chicken, quartered (about 3 pounds) *or* 3 pounds chicken pieces
⅓ cup honey
2 tablespoons fresh lime juice
1½ tablespoons reduced-sodium soy sauce
3 cups hot, cooked noodles (3½ ounces uncooked)

1. Preheat oven to 375°F. Arrange chicken, skin side up, in single layer in shallow casserole dish or 11 × 7-inch baking dish.

2. Combine remaining ingredients except noodles in small bowl; blend well. Brush one third of honey mixture over chicken; bake 15 minutes.

3. Brush remaining honey mixture over chicken; bake 10 to 15 minutes more or until juices run clear. Transfer to serving platter. Serve with noodles.   *Makes 4 servings*

SUPPERTIME DISHES

TURKEY MEDALLIONS WITH CUMBERLAND SAUCE

2½ teaspoons margarine, divided
¼ cup currant jelly
1½ tablespoons port wine
2 teaspoons lemon juice
¾ teaspoon prepared mustard
   Dash ground red pepper
1 teaspoon cornstarch
2 teaspoons cold water
1 Turkey Tenderloin (½ pound)
   Salt and black pepper
1 tablespoon olive oil
   Sour cream (optional)
   Fresh chives (optional)

1. In small saucepan, over medium-high heat, melt 1 teaspoon margarine. Stir in jelly, wine, lemon juice, mustard and ground red pepper; heat until jelly is melted.

2. In small bowl, combine cornstarch and water. Stir into jelly mixture. Boil until mixture is thickened. Reduce heat; keep warm.

3. Cut tenderloin into ¾-inch-thick crosswise slices to make medallions. Season with salt and black pepper.

4. In large skillet over medium-high heat, cook medallions in oil and remaining 1½ teaspoons margarine about 2½ minutes per side, or until no longer pink in centers.

5. To serve, spoon a thin layer of sauce on center of each plate. Arrange several turkey medallions over sauce. Garnish with sour cream and fresh chives, if desired. *Makes 2 servings*

Favorite recipe from **National Turkey Federation**

NO–PEEK SKILLET CHICKEN

2 tablespoons olive oil or vegetable oil
1 (2½- to 3-pound) broiler-fryer chicken, cut into serving pieces
1 can (14½ ounces) whole peeled tomatoes, undrained
1 jar (4½ ounces) sliced mushrooms, drained
1 clove garlic, minced
1 envelope LIPTON® Recipe Secrets® Onion Soup Mix*
   Hot cooked noodles (optional)
   Chopped fresh parsley (optional)

*Also terrific with LIPTON® Recipe Secrets® Beefy Mushroom Soup Mix.

In large skillet, heat oil over medium-high heat until hot. Add chicken; brown on all sides. Drain. Combine tomatoes with juice, mushrooms, garlic and onion soup mix in small bowl. Add to chicken in skillet. Simmer, covered, 45 minutes or until juices run clear. Serve with hot noodles and parsley, if desired. *Makes about 6 servings*

Turkey Medallions with Cumberland Sauce

SUPPERTIME DISHES

CHICKEN SMOTHERED IN ROASTED GARLIC WITH SWEET BASIL RED GRAVY

Roasted Garlic (recipe follows)
1 broiler-fryer chicken (about 3 pounds), cut into 8 pieces
2 tablespoons *plus* 2 teaspoons Chef Paul Prudhomme's® POULTRY MAGIC®, divided
1 cup all-purpose flour
2 cups vegetable oil or olive oil
2 cups finely chopped onions
3 bay leaves
1 cup finely chopped green bell peppers
3½ cups chopped peeled tomatoes
1 cup tomato sauce
3 tablespoons chopped fresh basil *or* 1½ teaspoons dried basil leaves
2 tablespoons firmly packed light brown sugar
3 cups chicken stock or water
½ teaspoon salt
Hot cooked rice (preferably converted) or pasta

Prepare Roasted Garlic; reserve. Season chicken with 1 tablespoon Poultry Magic®. Blend flour and 2 teaspoons Poultry Magic® in small bowl. Dust chicken pieces with seasoned flour. Heat oil in large skillet over high heat. Place chicken pieces in hot oil (large pieces first, skin side down) and brown 3 to 4 minutes on each side. When brown (chicken should not be fully cooked), remove chicken pieces from skillet and drain on paper towels. Pour off all but ¼ cup oil.

Reheat skillet and oil over high heat and add onions. Reduce heat to medium. Add 2 teaspoons Poultry Magic® and bay leaves; cook until onions are brown, stirring occasionally, about 5 minutes. Add bell peppers and cook 2 minutes, stirring occasionally.

Add tomatoes; increase heat to high and cook 1 minute. Stir in tomato sauce and basil and cook about 1 minute. Add reserved Roasted Garlic and cook about 1 minute. Stir in brown sugar; cook about 3 minutes. Add remaining 1 teaspoon Poultry Magic®; cook about 1 minute, then stir in stock.

Return chicken pieces to skillet and bring to a boil. Simmer, uncovered, about 25 minutes or until juices run clear, stirring occasionally to keep from sticking. Add salt and cook about 1 minute more. Remove bay leaves before serving. Serve with rice or pasta. *Makes 4 servings*

Roasted Garlic
35 unpeeled garlic cloves

Place unpeeled garlic cloves in single layer on baking sheet or in shallow baking pan. Do not crowd. Bake in preheated 400°F oven until outer leaves are dry-looking and edges start to turn brown, 12 to 15 minutes. Cool to room temperature and peel.

Chicken Smothered in Roasted Garlic with Sweet Basil Red Gravy

SUPPERTIME DISHES

BATTER–FRIED CHICKEN

1 (3-pound) broiler-fryer chicken, cut into
serving pieces
1 cup water
1 stalk celery (including leaves), cut into
2-inch pieces
1 small onion, cut into halves
1 clove garlic, cut into halves
½ teaspoon salt
⅛ teaspoon pepper
Fritter Batter (recipe follows)
Vegetable oil

1. Place chicken, water, celery, onion, garlic, salt and pepper in 5-quart Dutch oven; heat to a boil. Reduce heat to low; cover and simmer 20 to 25 minutes or until chicken is barely pink in center.

2. Meanwhile, prepare Fritter Batter. Remove chicken from Dutch oven. Drain and pat dry with paper towels. Cool slightly.

3. Heat 2½ to 3 inches oil in deep fryer or 5-quart Dutch oven over medium-high heat until oil registers 350°F.

4. Dip chicken in Fritter Batter to coat. Add several chicken pieces to oil. (Do not crowd; pieces should not touch.) Fry, turning occasionally, 5 to 7 minutes or until chicken is golden and is no longer pink in center.

5. Place fried chicken on cookie sheet lined with paper towels; keep warm in 200°F oven until ready to serve.   *Makes 4 servings*

Fritter Batter
1 cup all-purpose flour
1 teaspoon baking powder
1 teaspoon salt
¼ teaspoon white pepper
¾ cup milk
2 eggs
1 tablespoon vegetable oil

Combine flour, baking powder, salt and pepper in medium bowl; add milk, eggs and oil. Beat until well blended.   *Makes about 1¹/₂ cups*

CURRIED TURKEY DINNER

1 package (10 ounces) frozen broccoli
spears, cooked and drained
2 cups cubed Cooked Turkey
1 can (10½ ounces) reduced-sodium cream
of mushroom soup
¼ cup reduced-calorie mayonnaise
1½ teaspoons lemon juice
1 teaspoon curry powder
1 cup seasoned croutons

Preheat oven to 350°F. Place broccoli in 8-inch square baking dish; top with turkey. In small bowl, combine soup, mayonnaise, lemon juice and curry powder. Pour over turkey mixture; top with croutons. Bake 20 to 25 minutes or until bubbly.
            Makes 4 servings

*Favorite recipe from **National Turkey Federation***

Batter-Fried Chicken

SUPPERTIME DISHES

CHICKEN FAJITAS

8 (8-inch) flour tortillas
1 tablespoon vegetable oil
1 large green bell pepper, thinly sliced
1 large red bell pepper, thinly sliced
1 large onion, thinly sliced
1 clove garlic, minced
4 boneless skinless chicken breast halves
　　(about 1 pound), cut into ½-inch strips
½ teaspoon dried oregano leaves
2 tablespoons dry white wine or water
　　Salt and black pepper
　　Guacamole (optional)

1. Wrap tortillas in foil. Place in cold oven; set temperature to 350°F.

2. Heat oil in large skillet over medium-high heat. Add bell peppers, onion and garlic. Cook 3 to 4 minutes or until crisp-tender, stirring occasionally. Remove vegetable mixture with slotted spoon; set aside.

3. Add chicken to skillet; sprinkle with oregano. Cook 4 minutes or until chicken is no longer pink in center, stirring occasionally.

4. Return vegetable mixture to skillet. Add wine. Season with salt and black pepper; cover. Continue cooking 2 minutes or until thoroughly heated.

5. Fill warm tortillas with chicken mixture; serve with guacamole, if desired. *Makes 4 servings*

NOTE: To warm tortillas in microwave oven, wrap loosely in damp paper towel. Microwave on HIGH (100% power) 2 minutes or until hot.

DEEP-DISH TURKEY PIE

3 cups cubed cooked turkey or chicken
1 cup sliced cooked carrots
1 cup cubed cooked potatoes
1 cup frozen green peas, thawed
6 tablespoons margarine or butter
⅓ cup unsifted all-purpose flour
2 tablespoons WYLER'S® or STEERO®
　　Chicken-Flavor Instant Bouillon *or*
　　6 Chicken-Flavor Bouillon Cubes
¼ teaspoon pepper
4 cups BORDEN® or MEADOW GOLD® Milk
2¼ cups biscuit baking mix

Preheat oven to 375°F. In large saucepan, melt margarine; stir in flour, bouillon and pepper. Over medium heat, gradually add milk; cook and stir until bouillon dissolves and mixture thickens. Add remaining ingredients except biscuit mix; mix well.

Pour into 2½-quart baking dish. Prepare biscuit mix according to package directions for rolled biscuits. Roll out to cover dish; cut slashes in center of dough. Place on top of dish; crimp edges. Bake 40 minutes or until golden. Refrigerate leftovers. *Makes 6 servings*

Chicken Fajitas

CHICKEN ROSEMARY

 2 boneless skinless chicken breast halves
 1 teaspoon margarine
 1 teaspoon olive oil
    Salt and pepper
 ½ small onion, sliced
 1 large clove garlic, minced
 ½ teaspoon dried rosemary
 ⅛ teaspoon ground cinnamon
 ½ cup DOLE® Pine-Orange-Guava Juice
 1 tablespoon orange marmalade
 2 cups sliced DOLE® Carrots

Place chicken between 2 pieces of waxed paper or plastic wrap. Pound with flat side of meat mallet or rolling pin to ½-inch thickness. In medium skillet, brown chicken on both sides in margarine and oil. Sprinkle with salt and pepper. Stir in onion, garlic, rosemary and cinnamon. Cook and stir until onion is soft. Blend in juice and marmalade. Spoon over chicken. Cover; simmer 10 minutes. Stir in carrots. Cover; simmer 5 minutes or until carrots are tender-crisp and chicken is no longer pink in center. Garnish as desired.   *Makes 2 servings*

Prep time: 10 minutes
Cook time: 20 minutes

COQ AU VIN

 4 thin slices bacon, cut into ½-inch pieces
 6 chicken thighs, skinned
 ¾ teaspoon dried thyme leaves
    Salt and pepper (optional)
 1 large onion, coarsely chopped
 4 cloves garlic, minced
 ½ pound small red potatoes, quartered
10 mushrooms, quartered
 1 can (14½ ounces) DEL MONTE® Italian
    Recipe Stewed Tomatoes
 1½ cups dry red wine
    Chopped fresh parsley (optional)

In 4-quart heavy saucepan, cook and stir bacon over medium heat until just starting to brown. Sprinkle chicken with thyme; season with salt and pepper, if desired. Add chicken to pan; brown on all sides over medium-high heat. Add onion and garlic. Cook and stir 2 minutes; drain. Add potatoes, mushrooms, tomatoes and wine. Cook, uncovered, about 25 minutes or until potatoes are tender, sauce thickens and juices run clear, stirring occasionally. Garnish with parsley, if desired.

Makes 4 to 6 servings

Prep & Cook time: 45 minutes

Chicken Rosemary

SUPPERTIME DISHES

CHICKEN NORMANDY WITH NOODLES

2 whole boneless skinless chicken breasts (about 1 pound), halved
Salt and pepper
4 tablespoons butter or margarine, divided
¼ teaspoon dried thyme leaves
1 medium onion, chopped
1 large tart red apple, unpeeled and chopped
½ cup apple juice
2 tablespoons dry white wine (optional)
1½ cups water
½ cup milk
1 package LIPTON® Noodles & Sauce — Alfredo
2 tablespoons finely chopped fresh parsley

Lightly season chicken with salt and pepper. In large skillet, melt 2 tablespoons butter. Add chicken; sprinkle with thyme. Cook over medium-high heat until chicken is barely pink in center. Remove and keep warm. Add onion and apple to skillet; cook and stir until tender. Stir in apple juice and wine; simmer 2 minutes or until liquid is reduced by half. Return chicken to skillet. Simmer, covered, 5 minutes or until chicken is no longer pink in center.

Meanwhile, in medium saucepan, bring water, milk and remaining 2 tablespoons butter to a boil. Stir in noodles & Alfredo sauce. Continue boiling over medium heat, stirring occasionally, 8 minutes or until noodles are tender. Stir in parsley and pepper. To serve, arrange chicken over noodles.

Makes about 4 servings

TURKEY VEGETABLE MEDLEY

4 fresh turkey breast slices *or* 4 boneless skinless chicken breast halves
1 tablespoon vegetable oil
1 cup thin strips carrots
½ cup water
2 teaspoons WYLER'S® or STEERO® Chicken-Flavor Instant Bouillon *or* 2 Chicken-Flavor Bouillon Cubes
½ teaspoon dried thyme leaves or dried tarragon leaves
¼ teaspoon onion powder
1 cup *each* thin strips red and green bell peppers

In large skillet, brown turkey in oil. Add carrots, water, bouillon, thyme and onion powder. Cover; simmer 10 minutes. Add peppers; cover and cook 5 minutes longer or until peppers are tender and turkey is no longer pink in center. Garnish as desired. Refrigerate leftovers. *Makes 4 servings*

Turkey Vegetable Medley

MINI TURKEY LOAVES

1 pound ground turkey
1 small apple, chopped
½ small onion, chopped
½ cup uncooked rolled oats
2 teaspoons Dijon-style mustard
1 teaspoon dried rosemary leaves
1 teaspoon salt
Dash pepper
Cranberry sauce
Vegetable Stir-Fry (recipe follows)

Preheat oven to 425°F. Grease 12 (2½-inch) muffin cups. Combine turkey, apple, onion, oats, mustard, rosemary, salt and pepper in large bowl. Press into prepared muffin cups. Bake 20 minutes or until lightly browned and no longer pink in center. Remove from muffin cups; top with cranberry sauce. Garnish as desired. Serve with Vegetable Stir-Fry, if desired.   *Makes 4 servings*

Vegetable Stir-Fry

1 tablespoon vegetable oil
3 to 4 carrots, diagonally sliced
2 zucchini, diagonally sliced
3 tablespoons orange juice
Salt and pepper

Heat oil in medium skillet or wok over medium heat. Add carrots; stir-fry 3 minutes. Add zucchini and orange juice; stir-fry 4 minutes or until vegetables are crisp-tender. Season with salt and pepper to taste.

MEXICAN TURKEY RICE

½ cup chopped onion
⅓ cup long-grain rice
1 clove garlic, minced
1 tablespoon olive oil
1 can (16 ounces) low-salt stewed tomatoes, coarsely chopped
½ cup reduced-sodium chicken bouillon
1 teaspoon chili powder
½ teaspoon dried oregano leaves
⅛ teaspoon crushed red pepper
⅓ cup chopped green bell pepper
1 pound Fully-Cooked Oven-Roasted Turkey Breast, cut into ¼-inch cubes

1. In large nonstick skillet over medium-high heat, cook and stir onion, rice and garlic in oil 3 to 4 minutes or until rice is lightly browned. Stir in tomatoes, bouillon, chili powder, oregano and crushed red pepper. Bring to a boil. Reduce heat to low; cover and simmer 15 minutes.

2. Stir in bell pepper and turkey. Cover; cook 3 to 4 minutes or until mixture is heated through.
Makes 6 servings

*Favorite recipe from **National Turkey Federation***

Mini Turkey Loaves

FORTY–CLOVE CHICKEN FILICE

- 1 (3-pound) broiler-fryer chicken, cut into serving pieces
- 40 cloves garlic, peeled and left whole
- ½ cup dry white wine
- ¼ cup dry vermouth
- ¼ cup olive oil
- 4 ribs celery, thickly sliced
- 2 tablespoons finely chopped fresh parsley
- 2 teaspoons dried basil leaves
- 1 teaspoon dried oregano leaves
  Pinch crushed red pepper
- 1 lemon
  Salt and black pepper

Preheat oven to 375°F. Place chicken pieces, skin side up, in single layer in shallow baking pan. Combine garlic, wine, vermouth, oil, celery, parsley, basil, oregano and red pepper in medium bowl; mix thoroughly. Sprinkle garlic mixture over chicken pieces. Remove peel from lemon in thin strips; place peel over chicken mixture. Squeeze juice from lemon; sprinkle over chicken mixture. Season with salt and black pepper. Cover pan with aluminum foil. Bake 40 minutes. Remove foil; bake an additional 15 minutes or until juices run clear. Garnish as desired.   *Makes 4 to 6 servings*

Favorite recipe from **Christopher Ranch Garlic**

GOLDEN APPLE TURKEY SAUTÉ

- ½ pound boneless turkey
- 1 to 2 tablespoons vegetable oil
- 1 medium green bell pepper, sliced lengthwise into thin strips
- 1 medium onion, sliced lengthwise into thin strips
- 1 Golden Delicious apple, cored and thinly sliced
- 3 tablespoons vinegar
- 2 tablespoons sugar
- 1 tablespoon cornstarch
- 2 teaspoons soy sauce
- ½ teaspoon salt
  Dash black pepper

Remove skin from turkey; cut into 2½×½-inch strips. In large skillet, heat 1 tablespoon oil. Add turkey; cook and stir until no longer pink in center. Remove from pan. Add remaining 1 tablespoon oil to skillet, if necessary; cook and stir bell pepper and onion until crisp-tender. Return turkey to skillet; add apple and heat thoroughly. Combine remaining ingredients in small bowl. Add to turkey mixture; cook and stir until sauce thickens.

Makes 3 to 4 servings

Favorite recipe from **Washington Apple Commission**

Forty-Clove Chicken Filice

SUPPERTIME DISHES

BITTERSWEET FARM CHICKEN

- ½ cup all-purpose flour
- 1 teaspoon salt
- ¼ teaspoon pepper
- 1 (3½- to 4-pound) broiler-fryer chicken, cut into serving pieces
- 8 tablespoons butter or margarine, divided
- ¼ cup lemon juice
- ¼ cup orange-flavored liqueur
- ¼ cup honey
- 2 tablespoons grated orange peel
- 1 tablespoon soy sauce
  Whole cooked baby carrots

Preheat oven to 350°F. Combine flour, salt and pepper in large resealable plastic food storage bag. Add chicken pieces, a few at a time, to bag; shake to coat completely with flour mixture. Melt 4 tablespoons butter in large baking pan. Roll chicken in butter to coat all sides; arrange, skin side down, in single layer in pan. Bake 30 minutes.

Meanwhile, melt remaining 4 tablespoons butter in small saucepan over medium heat. Stir in lemon juice, liqueur, honey, orange peel and soy sauce; reserve 2 tablespoons mixture. Remove chicken from oven; turn pieces over. Pour remaining honey mixture over chicken. Continue baking, basting occasionally, 30 minutes or until chicken is glazed and juices run clear. Toss reserved honey mixture with cooked carrots; serve with chicken. Garnish as desired. *Makes 4 servings*

Favorite recipe from **National Broiler Council**

CALORIE–WISE DILL CHICKEN

- 1 cup plain low-fat yogurt
- 1½ cups regular wheat germ
- ½ cup chopped almonds
- 2 teaspoons dried dill weed
- ½ teaspoon salt
- ¼ teaspoon pepper
- 12 chicken drumsticks
  Nonstick vegetable cooking spray

Preheat oven to 350°F. Place yogurt in shallow bowl. Combine wheat germ, almonds, dill weed, salt and pepper in another shallow bowl. Dip chicken drumsticks, 1 at a time, into yogurt. Roll in wheat germ mixture to coat. Line baking sheet with aluminum foil; spray with nonstick vegetable cooking spray. Arrange chicken in a single layer on baking sheet. Bake about 50 minutes or until juices run clear. Garnish as desired.

Makes 4 servings

Favorite recipe from **National Broiler Council**

Calorie-Wise Dill Chicken

SUPPERTIME DISHES

CHICKEN PARMESAN

4 boneless skinless chicken breast halves
2 cans (14½ ounces each) DEL MONTE®
   Italian Recipe Stewed Tomatoes
2 tablespoons cornstarch
½ teaspoon dried oregano or basil leaves
¼ teaspoon hot pepper sauce (optional)
¼ cup grated Parmesan cheese
   Chopped parsley (optional)
   Hot cooked rice or pasta (optional)

Preheat oven to 425°F. Place chicken between 2 pieces of waxed paper or plastic wrap; pound with flat side of meat mallet or rolling pin to flatten slightly. Place in 11 × 7-inch baking dish. Cover with foil; bake 20 minutes or until chicken is no longer pink in center. Remove foil; drain. Meanwhile, in large saucepan, combine tomatoes, cornstarch, oregano and pepper sauce. Stir to dissolve cornstarch. Cook over medium-high heat, stirring constantly, until thickened. Pour sauce over chicken; top with cheese. Return to oven; bake, uncovered, 5 minutes or until cheese is melted. Garnish with chopped parsley and serve with rice or pasta, if desired.

Makes 4 servings

Prep & Cook time: 30 minutes

BUSY DAY TURKEY LOAF

1 cup KELLOGG'S® CROUTETTES®
   Stuffing Mix
½ cup skim milk
¼ cup finely chopped onion
2 egg whites
2 teaspoons Worcestershire sauce
½ teaspoon salt
1 pound lean ground turkey
¼ cup ketchup
2 teaspoons firmly packed brown sugar
1 teaspoon prepared mustard

1. Preheat oven to 350°F. Combine Kellogg's® Croutettes® Stuffing Mix and milk in large bowl. Let stand 5 minutes or until Croutettes® are softened. Add onion, egg whites, Worcestershire sauce and salt. Mix well. Add ground turkey. Mix until well combined.

2. Shape into loaf. Place in foil-lined shallow baking pan. Score loaf by making several diagonal grooves across top with spoon.

3. Combine ketchup, sugar and mustard in small bowl. Fill grooves with ketchup mixture.

4. Bake about 45 minutes or until browned and no longer pink in center. *Makes 6 servings*

Chicken Parmesan

SUPPERTIME DISHES

TURKEY–OLIVE RAGOÛT EN CRUST

½ **pound Boneless White or Dark Turkey Meat, cut into 1-inch cubes**
1 **clove garlic, minced**
1 **teaspoon vegetable oil**
¼ **cup (about 10) small whole frozen onions, thawed**
1 **medium red potato, unpeeled, cut into ½-inch cubes**
½ **cup reduced-sodium chicken bouillon or turkey broth**
½ **teaspoon dried parsley flakes**
⅛ **teaspoon dried thyme leaves**
1 **small bay leaf**
10 **frozen snow peas, thawed**
8 **whole, small pitted ripe olives**
1 **can (4 ounces) refrigerator crescent rolls**
½ **teaspoon dried dill weed**

1. Preheat oven to 375°F.

2. In medium skillet over medium heat, cook and stir turkey and garlic in oil 5 to 6 minutes or until turkey is no longer pink in center; remove and set aside. Add onions to skillet; cook and stir until lightly browned. Add potato, bouillon, parsley, thyme and bay leaf. Bring mixture to a boil. Reduce heat; cover and simmer 10 minutes or until potato is tender. Remove bay leaf.

3. Add turkey to potato mixture. Stir in snow peas and olives. Divide mixture between 2 (1¾-cup) casserole dishes.

4. Divide crescent rolls into 2 rectangles; press perforations together to seal. If necessary, roll out each rectangle to make dough large enough to cover top of casseroles. Sprinkle dough with dill weed, pressing lightly into dough. Cut small decorative shape from center of each dough piece; discard or place on baking sheet and bake in oven with casseroles. Place dough over casseroles; trim dough to fit. Press dough to edges of each casserole to seal. Bake 7 to 8 minutes or until dough is golden brown. *Makes 2 servings*

Lattice Crust: With a pastry wheel or knife, cut each dough rectangle into 6 lengthwise strips. Arrange strips, lattice-fashion, over each casserole; trim dough to fit. Press ends of dough to edges of each casserole to seal.

NOTE: For a more golden crust, brush top of dough with beaten egg yolk before baking.

Favorite recipe from **National Turkey Federation**

Turkey–Olive Ragoût en Crust

CHICKEN CURRY BOMBAY

1 medium onion, cut into wedges
2 cloves garlic, minced
2 teaspoons curry powder
1 tablespoon olive oil
2 boneless skinless chicken breast halves,
   sliced ¼ inch thick
1 can (14½ ounces) DEL MONTE® Original
   Recipe Stewed Tomatoes
⅓ cup DEL MONTE® Seedless Raisins
1 can (16 ounces) DEL MONTE® Whole New
   Potatoes, drained and cut into chunks
1 can (16 ounces) DEL MONTE® Blue Lake
   Cut Green Beans, drained
   Salt and pepper (optional)

In large skillet, cook onion, garlic and curry powder in oil over medium-high heat until onion is tender, stirring occasionally. Stir in chicken, tomatoes and raisins; bring to a boil. Reduce heat to medium; cover and simmer 8 minutes. Add potatoes and green beans. Cook, uncovered, 5 minutes, or until chicken is no longer pink in center, stirring occasionally. Season with salt and pepper, if desired. Garnish as desired.

Makes 4 servings

Prep time: 10 minutes
Cook time: 18 minutes

CHICKEN BREASTS WITH SAVORY MUSTARD HERB SAUCE

2 tablespoons vegetable oil, divided
4 boneless skinless chicken breast halves
   (about 1 pound)
1 medium zucchini, sliced
1½ cups sliced fresh or canned mushrooms
1 envelope LIPTON® Recipe Secrets®
   Savory Herb with Garlic or Golden
   Onion Soup Mix
¾ cup water
2 teaspoons country Dijon-style or brown
   prepared mustard

In large skillet, heat 1 tablespoon oil. Add chicken. Cook over medium heat 5 minutes or until chicken is barely pink in center, turning once; remove and keep warm.

In same skillet, heat remaining 1 tablespoon oil. Add zucchini and mushrooms; cook, stirring frequently, 3 minutes. Return chicken to skillet. Combine savory herb with garlic soup mix, water and mustard in small bowl; add to skillet. Bring to a boil; reduce heat and simmer, covered, 5 minutes or until chicken is no longer pink in center. To serve, arrange chicken on serving platter; top with vegetable and sauce mixture.

Makes about 4 servings

Chicken Curry Bombay

SUPPERTIME DISHES

CALIFORNIA ENCHILADAS

1 cup LIPTON® California Dip (recipe
   follows)
1 can (15 ounces) tomato sauce
1½ teaspoons hot pepper sauce, divided
½ teaspoon garlic powder
2 cups (8 ounces) shredded Monterey Jack
   or Muenster cheese, divided
1½ cups chopped cooked chicken
1 can (4 ounces) chopped green chilies,
   drained
12 corn tortillas, heated
1 large green bell pepper, cut into 12 thin
   strips

Preheat oven to 375°F. Prepare Lipton® California
Dip. Combine tomato sauce, ½ teaspoon hot
pepper sauce and garlic powder in small saucepan.
Bring to a boil over high heat. Reduce heat to low.
Simmer, uncovered, 15 minutes, stirring
occasionally. Combine 1½ cups cheese, chicken, 1
cup California Dip, chilies and remaining 1
teaspoon hot pepper sauce in large bowl. Spread
about 2½ tablespoons mixture on each tortilla; roll
up and place, seam side down, in lightly greased
12 × 8-inch baking dish. Top each tortilla with 1
tablespoon tomato sauce mixture, then sprinkle
remaining ½ cup cheese over tortillas. Top each
tortilla with bell pepper strip. Bake 15 minutes or
until cheese is melted. Serve with remaining
tomato sauce mixture.   *Makes 6 servings*

LIPTON® California Dip: Blend 1 envelope
LIPTON® Recipe Secrets® Onion Soup Mix with
1 pint (2 cups) sour cream in small bowl.
Refrigerate, covered, until chilled. Makes about
2 cups.

CHICKEN TERIYAKI KABOBS

1½ pounds chicken breasts, skinned and
   boned
8 (6-inch) bamboo skewers
1 bunch green onions, cut into 1-inch
   lengths
½ cup KIKKOMAN® Soy Sauce
2 tablespoons sugar
1 teaspoon vegetable oil
1 teaspoon minced fresh ginger
1 clove garlic, minced

Cut chicken into 1½-inch-square pieces. Thread
skewers alternately with chicken and green onion
pieces. (Spear green onion pieces crosswise.) Place
skewers in shallow pan. Combine soy sauce, sugar,
oil, ginger and garlic in small bowl; pour over
skewers. Brush chicken thoroughly with sauce.
Cover; marinate in refrigerator 30 minutes. Drain
marinade; reserve. Place skewers on rack of broiler
pan. Broil 3 minutes; turn over and brush with
reserved marinade. Broil for an additional 5
minutes or until chicken is no longer pink in
center.   *Makes 4 servings*

SUPPERTIME DISHES

CHICKEN PESTO MOZZARELLA

6 to 8 ounces uncooked linguine or corkscrew pasta
4 boneless skinless chicken breast halves
  Salt and pepper (optional)
1 tablespoon olive oil
1 can (14½ ounces) DEL MONTE® Recipe Pasta Style Chunky Tomatoes
½ medium onion, chopped
⅓ cup sliced pitted ripe olives
4 teaspoons pesto sauce,* divided
¼ cup (1 ounce) shredded skim-milk mozzarella cheese
  Hot cooked pasta (optional)

*Pesto sauce is available frozen or refrigerated at the supermarket.

Cook pasta according to package directions; drain. Meanwhile, season chicken with salt and pepper, if desired. In large skillet, brown chicken in oil over medium-high heat. Add tomatoes, onion and olives; bring to boil. Reduce heat to medium; cover and cook 8 minutes. Remove cover; cook over medium-high heat about 8 minutes or until chicken is no longer pink in center. Spread 1 teaspoon pesto over each breast; top with cheese. Cook, covered, until cheese melts. Serve over pasta, if desired.
Makes 4 servings

Prep time: 10 minutes
Cook time: 25 minutes

CHICKEN WITH LIME BUTTER

3 whole chicken breasts, split, skinned and boned
½ teaspoon salt
½ teaspoon pepper
⅓ cup vegetable oil
  Juice of 1 lime
½ cup butter
1 teaspoon minced chives
½ teaspoon dried dill weed

Sprinkle chicken with salt and pepper. Heat oil in large skillet over medium heat. Add chicken; cook until light brown, about 3 minutes per side. Cover; reduce heat to low. Cook 10 minutes or until chicken is no longer pink in center. Remove chicken to serving platter; keep warm.

Discard oil from skillet. Add lime juice; cook over low heat until juice begins to bubble, about 1 minute. Add butter, 1 tablespoon at a time, stirring until butter becomes opaque and forms a thickened sauce. Remove from heat; stir in chives and dill weed. Spoon sauce over chicken; serve immediately. Garnish as desired.
Makes 6 servings

*Favorite recipe from **National Broiler Council***

ENTERTAINING

CHICKEN CORDON BLEU

6 boneless skinless chicken breast halves
   (1¼ pounds)
1 tablespoon Dijon-style mustard
3 slices (1 ounce each) lean ham, cut into halves
3 slices (1 ounce each) reduced-fat Swiss cheese,
   cut into halves
   Nonstick cooking spray
¼ cup unseasoned dry bread crumbs
2 tablespoons minced fresh parsley
3 cups hot, cooked white rice

Preheat oven to 350°F. Place chicken between 2 pieces of waxed paper; pound to ¼-inch thickness using flat side of meat mallet or rolling pin. Brush mustard on 1 side of each chicken breast; layer 1 slice each of ham and cheese over mustard. Roll up each chicken breast from short end; secure with wooden picks. Spray tops of chicken rolls with cooking spray; sprinkle with bread crumbs. Arrange chicken rolls in 11 × 7-inch baking pan. Cover; bake 10 minutes. Uncover; bake about 20 minutes or until chicken is no longer pink in center. Stir parsley into rice; serve with chicken. Serve with vegetables, if desired. *Makes 6 servings*

GOURMET CHICKEN BAKE

   1 teaspoon seasoned salt
   ¼ teaspoon curry powder
   ¼ teaspoon dried savory leaves
   ¼ teaspoon white pepper
   3 whole chicken breasts, cut into halves
   1 cup buttermilk or sour milk*
   2 packages (6 ounces each) seasoned long-
        grain and wild rice
5½ cups chicken broth, divided
   1 pound fresh asparagus, trimmed
   2 tablespoons slivered almonds, toasted
   2 tablespoons chopped drained pimiento

*To sour milk, use 1 tablespoon lemon juice or vinegar plus enough milk to equal 1 cup. Stir; let stand 5 minutes before using.

Combine seasoned salt, curry powder, savory and pepper in small bowl. Sprinkle over chicken. Place chicken in large bowl; pour buttermilk over chicken. Cover; marinate in refrigerator overnight.

Preheat oven to 350°F. Drain chicken; reserve buttermilk marinade. Arrange chicken in single layer in 13 × 9-inch baking pan. Pour buttermilk marinade over chicken. Bake 1 hour or until juices run clear.

Cook rice according to package directions, substituting 5 cups chicken broth for water.

Meanwhile, cut asparagus 3 inches from tips, then cut remaining stalks into 1-inch pieces. Place asparagus tips and stalk pieces in remaining ¹/₂ cup broth in small saucepan. Cover and cook over medium heat 15 minutes or until tender. Set aside; do not drain.

Remove chicken from baking pan. Remove asparagus tips from saucepan; set aside.

Combine rice, asparagus stalk pieces and broth from asparagus in baking pan. Arrange chicken over rice mixture; place asparagus tips around chicken. Sprinkle with almonds and pimiento. Return to oven; bake about 10 minutes or until heated through.   *Makes 6 servings*

*Favorite recipe from **National Broiler Council***

Gourmet Chicken Bake

ENTERTAINING

DRESSED CHICKEN BREASTS WITH ANGEL HAIR PASTA

1 cup prepared HIDDEN VALLEY RANCH®
    Original Ranch® salad dressing
⅓ cup Dijon-style mustard
½ cup butter or margarine
4 whole chicken breasts, halved, skinned,
    boned and pounded thin
⅓ cup dry white wine
10 ounces angel hair pasta, cooked and
    drained
    Chopped fresh parsley
    Hot cooked asparagus (optional)

In small bowl, whisk together salad dressing and mustard; set aside. In medium skillet, melt butter over medium heat. Add chicken; cook until browned on both sides and no longer pink in center. Remove from skillet; keep warm. Pour wine into skillet; cook over medium-high heat about 5 minutes, scraping up any browned bits from bottom of skillet. Whisk in dressing mixture; blend well. Serve chicken over pasta; top with dressing mixture. Sprinkle with parsley. Serve with asparagus, if desired. *Makes 8 servings*

DIJON CHICKEN ELEGANT

4 whole boneless chicken breasts, split
⅓ cup GREY POUPON® Dijon or Country
    Dijon Mustard
1 teaspoon dried dill weed *or* 1 tablespoon
    chopped fresh dill
4 ounces Swiss cheese slices
2 frozen puff pastry sheets, thawed
1 egg white
1 tablespoon cold water

Preheat oven to 375°F. Place chicken, skin side down, between 2 pieces of waxed paper or plastic wrap; pound with flat side of meat mallet or rolling pin to ½-inch thickness. In small bowl, combine mustard and dill; spread over chicken breasts. Top each breast with cheese slice; trim to fit. Roll up chicken lengthwise, jelly-roll style.

Roll out each pastry sheet into 12-inch square; cut each into 4 (6-inch) squares. In small dish, beat egg white and water; brush edges of each square with egg mixture. Place 1 chicken roll diagonally on each square. Join 4 points of pastry over chicken; seal seams. Place on ungreased baking sheets. Brush with remaining egg mixture. Bake 30 minutes or until chicken reaches 185°F in center or is no longer pink. Serve immediately.
Makes 8 servings

Dressed Chicken Breasts with Angel Hair Pasta

ROAST TURKEY WITH PAN GRAVY

1 fresh or thawed frozen turkey (12 to 14 pounds); save giblets and neck for another use
Cornbread-Sausage Stuffing (recipe follows)
½ cup (1 stick) butter, melted
1 cup dry white wine or vermouth
3 tablespoons all-purpose flour
3 cups chicken broth
Salt and pepper

1. Preheat oven to 450°F. Rinse turkey; pat dry with paper towels. Stuff body and neck cavities loosely with stuffing. Fold skin over openings and close with skewers. Tie legs together with cotton string. Tuck wings under turkey.

2. Place turkey on meat rack in shallow roasting pan. Insert meat thermometer in thickest part of thigh, not touching bone. Brush one third of butter evenly over turkey.

3. Place turkey in oven; *immediately reduce oven temperature to 325°F.* Roast 22 to 24 minutes per pound for a total roasting time of 4 to 5½ hours. Brush with butter after 1 hour and again 1½ hours later. Baste with pan juices after each hour. If turkey starts overbrowning, tent with foil. Turkey is done when internal temperature reaches 180°F and legs move easily in sockets.

4. Transfer turkey to cutting board. Pour off juices from pan; reserve. Pour wine into pan and place over burners. Cook over medium-high heat, scraping up browned bits and stirring constantly, 2 to 3 minutes or until mixture is reduced by half.

5. Transfer ⅓ cup fat from pan juices to large saucepan. (Discard any remaining fat.) Add flour; cook and stir over medium heat 1 minute. Slowly stir in chicken broth, wine mixture and defatted pan juices. Cook over medium heat 10 minutes, stirring occasionally. Season with salt and pepper.
Makes 12 servings and 3½ cups gravy

Cornbread-Sausage Stuffing

8 ounces bulk pork sausage (regular or spicy)
½ cup butter or margarine
2 medium onions, chopped
2 cloves garlic, minced
2 teaspoons dried sage
1 teaspoon poultry seasoning
1 package (16 ounces) prepared dry cornbread crumbs
¾ cup chicken broth

1. Brown sausage in large skillet over medium-high heat until no longer pink, stirring to separate meat. Drain sausage on paper towels; set aside. Pour off grease from skillet.

2. Melt butter in same skillet over medium heat until foamy. Cook and stir onions and garlic in butter until onions are softened, about 10 minutes. Stir in sage and poultry seasoning; cook 1 minute more. Combine cornbread crumbs, sausage and onion mixture in large bowl. Drizzle broth over stuffing; toss lightly until evenly moistened.
Makes 12 cups stuffing

Roast Turkey with Pan Gravy

ENTERTAINING

CHICKEN WITH FRUIT AND MIXED MUSTARDS

½ **cup Dijon-style mustard**
½ **cup Bavarian or other German mustard**
1 **tablespoon Chinese mustard**
⅓ **cup honey**
⅓ **cup light cream**
2 **whole chicken breasts, split, skinned and boned**
½ **teaspoon salt**
¼ **teaspoon pepper**
2 **tablespoons butter or margarine**
4 **kiwifruit, peeled and sliced**
1 **cup honeydew melon balls**
1 **cup cantaloupe balls**
¼ **cup mayonnaise**
    Mint sprigs (optional)

Combine mustards, honey and cream in medium bowl. Spoon half the mustard mixture into large glass bowl; reserve remainder. Sprinkle chicken with salt and pepper; place in glass bowl, turning to coat with mustard mixture. Cover; marinate in refrigerator 30 minutes, turning often.

Heat butter in large skillet over medium heat until foamy. Remove chicken from mustard mixture; discard mustard mixture from bowl. Add chicken to skillet; cook about 7 minutes on each side or until browned and no longer pink in center. Remove chicken to cutting board; cut across the grain into thin slices. Arrange chicken and fruit on serving platter.

Place reserved mustard mixture in small saucepan; whisk in mayonnaise. Heat thoroughly over medium heat. Drizzle a portion of mustard mixture over chicken; serve with remaining mustard mixture. Garnish platter with mint sprigs, if desired. *Makes 4 servings*

Favorite recipe from Delmarva Poultry Industry, Inc.

EURASIAN ROASTED CHICKEN

1 **(3- to 3½-pound) whole frying chicken**
¼ **cup KIKKOMAN® Soy Sauce**
3 **tablespoons Burgundy wine**
3 **tablespoons olive oil**
2 **cloves garlic, minced**
1½ **teaspoons dried marjoram leaves**
¾ **teaspoon pepper**

Preheat oven to 350°F. Remove and discard giblets and neck from chicken. Rinse chicken under cold water; drain well and pat dry with paper towels. Place chicken, breast side up, in shallow roasting pan. Blend soy sauce, wine, olive oil, garlic, marjoram and pepper in small bowl. Brush body and cavity thoroughly with sauce mixture. Roast 1 hour and 30 minutes or until chicken juices run clear and legs move freely, brushing chicken with sauce mixture every 30 minutes. Let stand 10 minutes before carving. Discard any remaining sauce. *Makes 4 servings*

Chicken with Fruit and Mixed Mustards

LIGHT–STYLE LEMON CHICKEN

2 egg whites, slightly beaten
¾ cup fresh bread crumbs
2 tablespoons sesame seeds (optional)
¾ teaspoon salt
¼ teaspoon black pepper
4 boneless skinless chicken breast halves (about 1¼ pounds)
2 tablespoons all-purpose flour
¾ cup canned chicken broth
4 teaspoons cornstarch
¼ cup fresh lemon juice
2 tablespoons firmly packed brown sugar
1 tablespoon honey
2 tablespoons vegetable oil
4 cups thinly sliced napa cabbage or lettuce
Lemon slices (optional)
Fresh herbs (optional)

Place egg whites in shallow dish. Combine bread crumbs, sesame seeds, salt and pepper in another shallow dish. Dust chicken with flour. Dip one chicken breast into beaten egg whites. Then roll in bread crumb mixture to coat. Repeat with remaining chicken breasts.

Blend broth into cornstarch in small bowl until smooth. Stir in lemon juice, brown sugar and honey. Set aside.

Heat oil in large nonstick skillet over medium heat until hot. Add chicken; cook 5 minutes. Turn chicken over; cook 5 to 6 minutes or until browned and no longer pink in center. Transfer to cutting board; keep warm.

Wipe skillet clean with paper towel. Stir broth mixture; add to skillet. Cook and stir 3 to 4 minutes or until sauce boils and thickens.

Place cabbage on serving dish. Cut chicken crosswise into ½-inch slices; place over cabbage. Pour sauce over chicken. Garnish with lemon slices and fresh herbs, if desired.   *Makes 4 servings*

Light-Style Lemon Chicken

CLASSIC CHICKEN MARSALA

- 2 tablespoons unsalted butter
- 1 tablespoon vegetable oil
- 4 boneless skinless chicken breast halves (about 1¼ pounds)
- 4 slices mozzarella cheese (1 ounce each)
- 12 capers, drained
- 4 flat anchovy fillets, drained
- 1 tablespoon chopped fresh parsley
- 1 clove garlic, minced
- 3 tablespoons Marsala wine
- ⅔ cup heavy or whipping cream
- Dash *each* salt and pepper
- Hot cooked pasta (optional)

Heat butter and oil in large skillet over medium-high heat until melted and bubbly. Add chicken; reduce heat to medium. Cook, uncovered, 5 to 6 minutes per side or until chicken is golden brown. Remove from heat. Top each chicken breast with 1 cheese slice, 3 capers and 1 anchovy fillet.

Return skillet to heat. Sprinkle chicken with parsley. Cover and cook over low heat 3 minutes or until cheese is semi-melted and chicken is no longer pink in center. Remove chicken with slotted spatula to serving dish; keep warm.

Add garlic to drippings remaining in skillet; cook and stir over medium heat 30 seconds. Stir in wine; cook and stir 45 seconds, scraping up any brown bits in skillet. Stir in cream. Cook and stir 3 minutes or until sauce thickens slightly. Stir in salt and pepper. Spoon sauce over chicken. Serve with pasta. Garnish as desired.   *Makes 4 servings*

CHICKEN CACCIATORE

- 1 pound boneless skinless chicken breasts, cut into strips
- ½ cup chopped onion
- 1 medium green bell pepper, cut into strips
- 1 clove garlic, minced
- 2 tablespoons oil
- 1 can (28 ounces) whole tomatoes
- 1 can (8 ounces) tomato sauce
- ½ teaspoon salt
- ½ teaspoon dried oregano leaves
- ½ teaspoon dried basil leaves
- ⅛ teaspoon ground red pepper (optional)
- 1½ cups MINUTE® Original Rice, uncooked

Cook and stir chicken, onion, bell pepper and garlic in hot oil in large skillet until lightly browned and chicken is barely pink in center. Add remaining ingredients except rice. Bring to a boil. Stir in rice. Cover; remove from heat. Let stand 5 minutes. Fluff with fork.   *Makes 4 servings*

MICROWAVE DIRECTIONS: Combine chicken, onion, bell pepper, garlic and oil in large microwavable dish. Cover; cook at HIGH (100% power) 5 minutes. Stir in remaining ingredients. Cover; cook at HIGH an additional 5 to 6 minutes or until chicken is no longer pink in center. Let stand 5 minutes. Fluff with fork.

Classic Chicken Marsala

CHICKEN DIANE

6 ounces uncooked pasta
Vegetable oil
¾ cup (1½ sticks) unsalted butter, softened, divided
1 tablespoon *plus* 2 teaspoons Chef Paul Prudhomme's® POULTRY MAGIC®
¾ pound boneless skinless chicken breasts, cut into strips
3 cups sliced mushrooms (about 8 ounces)
1 cup chicken stock or water
¼ cup minced green onion tops
3 tablespoons minced fresh parsley
1 teaspoon minced garlic

Cook pasta according to package directions. Drain; rinse with hot water to wash off starch, then with cold water to stop cooking process. Drain again. To prevent pasta from sticking together, toss pasta with a very small amount of oil. Set aside.

Combine 4 tablespoons butter and Poultry Magic® in medium bowl. Heat large skillet over high heat until hot, about 4 minutes. Add butter mixture. Add chicken strips to melted butter mixture. Cook and stir 3 minutes or until chicken is browned. Add mushrooms and cook and stir 2 minutes. Add stock, green onions, parsley and garlic. Cook 2 minutes more or until sauce boils rapidly. Cut remaining ½ cup butter into pats; add to sauce mixture, stirring and shaking pan to incorporate. Cook 3 minutes and add cooked pasta. Stir and shake pan to mix well. Serve immediately. Garnish as desired. *Makes 2 servings*

ORANGE–GLAZED TURKEY BREAST WITH RAISIN–ALMOND WILD RICE

½ bone-in skinless turkey breast (about 2½ pounds)
1 tablespoon olive oil or vegetable oil
Salt and pepper
½ cup *plus* 2 tablespoons orange marmalade, divided
1 tablespoon finely shredded fresh ginger
2⅓ cups water
1 tablespoon butter or margarine
1 package (6 ounces) UNCLE BEN'S® Long Grain & Wild Rice Original Recipe
⅓ cup raisins
⅓ cup toasted slivered almonds

Preheat oven to 400°F. Brush turkey with oil; sprinkle with salt and pepper. Combine ½ cup marmalade and ginger in small bowl; set aside. Place turkey on rack in shallow foil-lined roasting pan. Roast 30 minutes. Brush ⅓ of marmalade mixture evenly over turkey. Continue to roast 25 to 35 minutes or until meat thermometer inserted in thickest part registers 170°F, brushing twice with remaining marmalade mixture. Meanwhile, combine water, butter, contents of rice and seasoning packets, raisins and remaining 2 tablespoons marmalade in medium saucepan. Bring to a boil. Reduce heat; cover tightly and simmer until all water is absorbed, about 25 minutes. Slice turkey. Stir almonds into rice; serve alongside turkey. *Makes 6 servings*

Chicken Diane

ENTERTAINING

OLYMPIC SEOUL CHICKEN

¼ **cup white vinegar**
3 **tablespoons soy sauce**
2 **tablespoons honey**
¼ **teaspoon ground ginger**
2 **tablespoons peanut oil**
8 **chicken thighs, skinned**
10 **cloves garlic, coarsely chopped**
½ **to 1 teaspoon crushed red pepper**
2 **ounces Chinese rice stick noodles,**
    cooked *or* 2 **cups hot cooked rice**
    Snow peas, steamed
    Diagonally sliced yellow squash, steamed

Combine vinegar, soy sauce, honey and ginger in small bowl; set aside. Heat oil in large skillet over medium-high heat. Add chicken; cook about 10 minutes or until evenly browned on all sides. Add garlic and red pepper; cook, stirring frequently, 2 to 3 minutes. Drain off excess fat. Add vinegar mixture. Cover; reduce heat and simmer about 15 minutes or until juices run clear. Uncover; cook about 2 minutes or until sauce has reduced and thickened. Serve with rice stick noodles, peas and squash. Garnish as desired. *Makes 4 servings*

Favorite recipe from Delmarva Poultry Industry, Inc.

CHICKEN SALTIMBOCCA

3 **whole boneless skinless chicken breasts,**
    cut in half
6 **thin slices prosciutto or ham**
6 **thin slices mozzarella cheese**
3 **teaspoons dried basil leaves, divided**
1½ **teaspoons LAWRY'S® Garlic Powder with**
    Parsley, divided
¾ **cup plain dry bread crumbs**
1 **teaspoon LAWRY'S® Seasoned Pepper**
3 **to 4 tablespoons IMPERIAL® Margarine**

Pound chicken breasts between 2 sheets of waxed paper or plastic wrap to ¼-inch thickness with flat side of meat mallet or rolling pin. Place 1 slice prosciutto and 1 slice mozzarella cheese on each breast; trim to fit. Sprinkle each with ½ teaspoon basil and ¼ teaspoon Garlic Powder with Parsley. Roll up lengthwise, jelly-roll style, tucking ends in. Secure each with wooden toothpick. In medium bowl, combine bread crumbs and Seasoned Pepper; blend well. Coat chicken with crumb mixture. In large nonstick skillet, melt margarine over medium heat; brown chicken on all sides. Cover; cook 25 to 30 minutes or until chicken is no longer pink in center and cheese is melted. Remove toothpicks before serving.

Makes 6 servings

PRESENTATION: Serve with garlic-butter linguine and steamed zucchini.

Olympic Seoul Chicken

ENTERTAINING

APRICOT CHICKEN ORIENTAL

1 tablespoon butter or margarine
2 whole chicken breasts, split, skinned and
  boned
1 jar (10 ounces) apricot preserves
1 cup water
½ cup soy sauce
1 can (8 ounces) sliced water chestnuts,
  drained and liquid reserved
12 dried apricots, coarsely chopped
1 teaspoon ground ginger
1 teaspoon garlic powder
  Apricot Rice (recipe follows)
3 ribs celery, diagonally sliced
2 cups sliced mushrooms
1 bunch green onions, sliced
1 package (6 ounces) frozen pea pods
1 red or green bell pepper, cut into strips

Melt butter in large skillet over medium heat. Add chicken; cook until brown on both sides. Stir in preserves, water, soy sauce, liquid from water chestnuts, apricots, ginger and garlic powder. Simmer 40 minutes or until chicken is no longer pink in center. Meanwhile, prepare Apricot Rice. Add vegetables to skillet; cook and stir 5 minutes or until heated through. Serve over Apricot Rice. Garnish as desired. *Makes 4 servings*

Apricot Rice: Combine 2½ cups water, ¼ cup finely chopped dried apricots and ¼ teaspoon salt in medium saucepan. Bring to a boil; stir in 1 cup long-grain rice. Cover; reduce heat and simmer 20 minutes. Remove from heat; let stand 5 minutes.

Favorite recipe from **California Apricot Advisory Board**

SESAME BAKED CHICKEN WITH PEA POD WILD RICE

3 whole chicken breasts, split, skinned and
  boned
  Salt
¼ cup *plus* 1 tablespoon honey, divided
2 tablespoons firmly packed brown sugar
2 to 3 teaspoons finely shredded fresh
  ginger
1 tablespoon lightly toasted sesame seeds
2⅓ cups water
1 tablespoon butter or margarine
1 package (6 ounces) UNCLE BEN'S® Long
  Grain & Wild Rice Original Recipe
2 cups pea pods, halved if large
½ cup sliced green onions with tops

Preheat oven to 350°F. Sprinkle chicken with salt. Combine ¼ cup honey, brown sugar and ginger in small bowl; mix well. Brush over all sides of chicken; place chicken in single layer in shallow baking dish. Sprinkle evenly with sesame seeds. Bake 25 minutes or until chicken is no longer pink in center.

Meanwhile, combine water, butter and contents of rice and seasoning packets in medium saucepan. Bring to a boil. Reduce heat; cover tightly and simmer 22 minutes. Stir in pea pods; cover and continue to simmer until all water is absorbed, about 3 minutes. Stir green onions and remaining 1 tablespoon honey into rice mixture; serve with chicken. *Makes 6 servings*

Apricot Chicken Oriental

ENTERTAINING

LEMON CHICKEN AND RICE

1 pound boneless skinless chicken breasts,
    cut into strips
1 medium onion, chopped
2 cloves garlic, minced
2 tablespoons margarine or butter
1 can (13¾ ounces) chicken broth
1 tablespoon cornstarch
1 large carrot, diagonally sliced
½ teaspoon grated lemon peel
2 tablespoons fresh lemon juice
½ teaspoon salt
1½ cups MINUTE® Original Rice, uncooked
1 cup fresh snow pea pods *or* 1 package
    (6 ounces) frozen snow pea pods
3 tablespoons chopped fresh parsley

Cook and stir chicken, onion and garlic in hot margarine in large skillet until chicken is lightly browned. Combine broth and cornstarch in small bowl; stir into chicken mixture.

Add carrot, lemon peel, lemon juice and salt. Cook and stir until mixture thickens and comes to a full boil. Stir in rice, snow pea pods and parsley. Cover; remove from heat. Let stand 5 minutes. Fluff with fork.

Makes 4 servings

CHICKEN BREASTS FLORENTINE

2 pounds boneless skinless chicken
    breasts
¼ cup all-purpose flour
2 eggs, well beaten
⅔ cup seasoned dry bread crumbs
1 envelope LIPTON® Recipe Secrets®
    Golden Onion Soup Mix
1½ cups water
¼ cup dry white wine
1 clove garlic, finely chopped
2 tablespoons finely chopped fresh parsley
⅛ teaspoon pepper
    Hot cooked rice pilaf or white rice
    Hot cooked spinach

To Microwave: Dip chicken in flour, then eggs, then bread crumbs. In 3-quart microwave-safe casserole, microwave chicken, uncovered, at HIGH (100% power) 4 minutes, rearranging chicken once. Combine golden onion soup mix, water, wine and garlic in small bowl; add to chicken. Microwave, uncovered, at HIGH 5 minutes or until boiling, stirring once. Microwave, uncovered, at MEDIUM (50% power), stirring occasionally, 7 minutes or until chicken is no longer pink in center and sauce is slightly thickened. Stir in parsley and pepper. Let stand, covered, 5 minutes. To serve, arrange chicken over hot rice and spinach; garnish as desired.

Makes about 6 servings

GREEK ISLAND CHICKEN

- 1 (3-pound) broiler-fryer chicken, cut into serving pieces
- 1 quart water
- 1 lemon, thinly sliced
- 2 tablespoons chopped chives
- 1 tablespoon lime juice
- 1¼ teaspoons salt, divided
- 10 peppercorns
- 4 juniper berries, crushed
- 3 whole cloves
- ⅛ teaspoon dried rosemary
- ⅛ teaspoon ground cinnamon
- 1 small bay leaf
- ⅓ cup finely chopped onion
- 1 clove garlic, minced
- 3 tablespoons olive oil
- 1 cup chopped fresh tomatoes
- ½ teaspoon ground coriander
- ¼ teaspoon pepper
- 3 tablespoons white wine
- 2 tablespoons sliced pitted ripe olives
- ¼ cup crumbled feta cheese
- 2 tablespoons dry bread crumbs

*Prior to heating, chicken mixture may be covered and refrigerated several hours or overnight. To heat, cover with foil. Bake at 350°F for 20 minutes. Remove foil; bake an additional 10 minutes or until heated through.

Place chicken, water, lemon, chives, lime juice, 1 teaspoon salt, peppercorns, juniper berries, cloves, rosemary, cinnamon and bay leaf in large saucepan. Bring to a boil over high heat. Reduce heat to low. Cover and simmer 30 minutes or until chicken is no longer pink in center. Remove from heat. Cool chicken in stock about 15 minutes. Remove chicken; skim fat from broth. Strain broth; reserve ¼ cup broth. Remove meat from bones, discarding bones and skin. Chop chicken into bite-sized pieces. Arrange chicken in greased shallow baking dish.

Preheat oven to 350°F. Cook and stir onion and garlic in hot oil in medium skillet over low heat until onion is transparent. Stir in tomatoes, coriander, remaining ¼ teaspoon salt and pepper. Cook and stir an additional 3 minutes. Add wine, olives and reserved broth; pour over chicken. Combine feta cheese and bread crumbs in small bowl. Sprinkle over chicken. Bake 15 minutes or until heated through.*   *Makes 4 servings*

Favorite recipe from **National Broiler Council**

——Acknowledgments——

The publishers would like to thank the companies and organizations listed below for the use of their recipes and photos in this publication.

Best Foods, a Division of CPC
    International Inc.
Blue Diamond Growers
Borden Kitchens, Borden, Inc.
California Apricot Advisory Board
California Poultry Industry
    Federation
Chef Paul Prudhomme's Magic
    Seasoning Blends
Christopher Ranch Garlic
The Creamette Company
Delmarva Poultry Industry, Inc.
Del Monte Corporation
Dole Food Company, Inc.
Heinz U.S.A.
The HVR Company
Kellogg Company
Kikkoman International Inc.

The Kingsford Products Company
Kraft Foods, Inc.
Lawry's® Foods, Inc.
Thomas J. Lipton Co.
Louis Rich Company
McIlhenny Company
Nabisco Foods Group
National Broiler Council
National Dairy Board
National Turkey Federation
Nestlé Food Company
Perdue® Farms
Ralston Foods, Inc.
Uncle Ben's Rice
USA Rice Council
Washington Apple Commission
Wisconsin Milk Marketing Board

Index

– Index –

METRIC CONVERSION CHART

VOLUME MEASUREMENTS (dry)

$\frac{1}{8}$ teaspoon = 0.5 mL
$\frac{1}{4}$ teaspoon = 1 mL
$\frac{1}{2}$ teaspoon = 2 mL
$\frac{3}{4}$ teaspoon = 4 mL
1 teaspoon = 5 mL
1 tablespoon = 15 mL
2 tablespoons = 30 mL
$\frac{1}{4}$ cup = 60 mL
$\frac{1}{3}$ cup = 75 mL
$\frac{1}{2}$ cup = 125 mL
$\frac{2}{3}$ cup = 150 mL
$\frac{3}{4}$ cup = 175 mL
1 cup = 250 mL
2 cups = 1 pint = 500 mL
3 cups = 750 mL
4 cups = 1 quart = 1 L

VOLUME MEASUREMENTS (fluid)

1 fluid ounce (2 tablespoons) = 30 mL
4 fluid ounces ($\frac{1}{2}$ cup) = 125 mL
8 fluid ounces (1 cup) = 250 mL
12 fluid ounces (1$\frac{1}{2}$ cups) = 375 mL
16 fluid ounces (2 cups) = 500 mL

WEIGHTS (mass)

$\frac{1}{2}$ ounce = 15 g
1 ounce = 30 g
3 ounces = 90 g
4 ounces = 120 g
8 ounces = 225 g
10 ounces = 285 g
12 ounces = 360 g
16 ounces = 1 pound = 450 g

DIMENSIONS

$\frac{1}{16}$ inch = 2 mm
$\frac{1}{8}$ inch = 3 mm
$\frac{1}{4}$ inch = 6 mm
$\frac{1}{2}$ inch = 1.5 cm
$\frac{3}{4}$ inch = 2 cm
1 inch = 2.5 cm

OVEN TEMPERATURES

250°F = 120°C
275°F = 140°C
300°F = 150°C
325°F = 160°C
350°F = 180°C
375°F = 190°C
400°F = 200°C
425°F = 220°C
450°F = 230°C

BAKING PAN SIZES

Utensil	Size in Inches/Quarts	Metric Volume	Size in Centimeters
Baking or Cake Pan (square or rectangular)	8×8×2	2 L	20×20×5
	9×9×2	2.5 L	22×22×5
	12×8×2	3 L	30×20×5
	13×9×2	3.5 L	33×23×5
Loaf Pan	8×4×3	1.5 L	20×10×7
	9×5×3	2 L	23×13×7
Round Layer Cake Pan	8×1½	1.2 L	20×4
	9×1½	1.5 L	23×4
Pie Plate	8×1¼	750 mL	20×3
	9×1¼	1 L	23×3
Baking Dish or Casserole	1 quart	1 L	—
	1½ quart	1.5 L	—
	2 quart	2 L	—